Crystal Ball

Crystal Ball

Stones, Amulets, and Talismans *for*
Power, Protection, and Prophecy

Sibyl Ferguson

Revised and expanded by Witch Bree

WEISER BOOKS
Boston, MA/York Beach, ME

This edition first published in 2005 by
Red Wheel/Weiser, LLC
York Beach, ME
With offices at:
368 Congress Street
Boston, MA 02210
www.redwheelweiser.com

Library of Congress Cataloging-in-Publication Data
Ferguson, Sibyl.
  Crystal ball : stones, amulets, and talismans of power, protection,
and
prophecy / Sibyl Ferguson.—Rev. and expanded.
     p. cm.
  Includes bibliographical references.
  ISBN 1-57863-348-6
  1. Crystal gazing. 2. Crystals— Psychic aspects. I. Title.
  BF1335.F47 2005
  133'.2548--dc22
                        2004027266

Typeset in Novarese Book 10/14 by Garrett Brown

Printed in Canada
FR

12 11 10 09 08 07 06 05
  8 7 6 5 4 3 2 1

Contents

Introduction

This book is an invitation to use the power of crystals and gem-stones to transform your life. Part 1 is Sibyl Ferguson's original text of *The Crystal Ball*. In it, she reveals the history of the crystal ball as a divining tool and shows you how to care for and house your crystal ball as well as interpret the various phenomena you might see as you gaze into it.

Part 2 builds on Sibyl's excellent foundation of research and recommendations. It's filled with fascinating and informative crystal lore and numerous suggestions for using crystals to heal your body, feed your spirit, and enhance your psychic abilities as well as bring abundance, love, and personal protection into your life.

Each special stone carries with it a power and a blessing you can use to create a life of abundance, good health, and spiritual well-being, and *Crystal Ball* will help you find the stones that are right for you.

Part I

The Crystal Ball

Sibyl Ferguson

While the crystal ball is a little understood mode of divination, it is one method, if not the most enticing, of augury. Probably there are as many definitions of crystal balls as there are opinionated people. However, it is usual to group these individuals into three categories—the ancients; the geologists; and the seers, or scryers.

The ancients supposed crystals to be congealed water or ice petrified by some long-continued natural process. These long-ago people invoked the power of the crystal to change the fate of individuals, and often to modify the course of a country's events. It is reported that Pliny the Elder (23–79) subscribed to this belief, and that Seneca (4 B.C.?–65 A.D.) supported his opinion. This belief extended well into the Middle Ages. Even today under the tundra of North America may be found a buried sheet of ice formed by clear spring water, which rises from the rocks beneath the alluvial deposits at the Zone of Freezing. This crystosphene, as it is designated, might easily deceive individuals today, had not the ancients' belief been refuted by the geologists.

The geologist, to put it briefly and simply, is a person who specializes in the history of the earth as recorded in the rocks. The geologist defines a crystal as a body formed by the solidification of a chemical or compound. It is either colorless or only slightly tinged with color. It is known as quartz or rock-crystal. The geologist is a very practical person who, generally, does not lean toward the occult. To him a crystal is a crystal is a crystal. True, but is there anyone who is able to forget that magical device—the first radio? It was known as a *crystal* set for its receiver had a crystal detector. All instruments worthy of being classed as magical do affect the future of humanity. Need it be pointed out to anyone the undreamed future of that original crystal radio set?

The seer, or scryer, sees the crystal ball very differently. He looks upon it as the Generic Ovum in whose transparent, unfathomable depth lies the whole of creation. In it is preserved all terrestrial energy in its myriad forms. The seer is a person credited with extraordinary moral and spiritual insight and practices crystallomancy, or divination, through gazing into the crystal ball.

Health and the Crystal Ball

One of the first concerns confronting those desirous of becoming seers is health. The vigor and robustness of an athlete are *not* a requisite. The essentials are a reasonably sound mind and body. To attain a reliable and high stage of perception, a healthy brain, a steady heart, and lungs capable of deep breathing are indispensable. The scryer remains calm and unmoved by trivialities under any circumstance.

Extensive observation by reliable medical men has shown conclusively that crystal gazing has no ill effect on the scryer's health. One of the most renowned scryers, Miss Goodrich-Freer, is quoted as saying, "The four years during which I have carried on experiments in crystal-gazing have been among the healthiest of my life."

The writings of some of the great occultists have presented a similar opinion. To name two, both F. Podmore and F.W.H. Myers felt crystal gazing had no adverse effect on the health of the seer. Their continued investigations along with those of other reputable authors presented a most encouraging picture. As the seer's development progressed, uncertainty or apparent discomfort was replaced by a stable, serene attitude. The mental efficiency was unmistakably enhanced.

Where and How to House the Crystal Ball

A crystal ball is not a toy, and it should be treated with great respect and deference. If the owner is seriously considering seership, it is important to house the Crystal Ball in a room of its own. A small room is preferable, and it should be kept impeccably clean. This applies to the entire room—floors, walls, and windows, as well as the furnishings. Anything that might distract the attention should be eliminated.

The furnishings should be kept simple and down to a minimum. A small, sturdy table to hold the crystal ball and two unpretentious but comfortable chairs should be sufficient. However, if the seer finds it necessary to record what the crystal ball has revealed, a small chest of drawers to accommodate stationery may be added.

Keep the crystal ball clean! This is not a rule. It is a *command*. When its surface becomes soiled, make a mild solution of luke-warm water and triple-milled soap in a small basin. Rest the crystal ball on a square of white flannel, which has been placed on the bottom of the basin. Gently wash the crystal ball to remove all trace of soil. Then rinse in a solution of alcohol and water, or preferably a solution of vinegar and water. Dry with a soft linen cloth, and polish with a piece of chamois kept for that purpose.

As has been said already, the crystal ball is not a toy to be handled indiscriminately by anyone out of curiosity. Ideally, only the seer's hands should touch it. The dedicated scryer magnetizes the crystal ball by passing the right hand over it to impart strength and might. Then the action should be repeated with the left hand to transmit more sensitiveness. Generally, when the seer is alone this exercise is carried on for five minutes at several periods during the day. Then, too, magnetism from the transcendental ethers collect on the surface of the crystal ball as the seer gazes fixedly upon it. To put it simply in the words of the modern idiom, this is comparable to "recharging the battery."

It can be readily understood that handling by the curious actually destroys the sensitiveness of the crystal ball. As has been pointed out, magnetism collects on the surface of this extremely responsive instrument. However, it is conceded that the crystal ball is an inanimate object. It is powerless to say, "I shall allow only the seer's magnetism to collect on my surface." It is unable to move away from an alien intruder. Its power is to reveal to a sensitive that which lies quietly in its heart.

It is acknowledged that handling leaves magnetic vibrations that, mingled with the seer's, cause much confusion that is not only worthless but detrimental to all concerned. If a person is equipped to become a consulting scryer, then that person must be strong enough to firmly but kindly refuse to allow the crystal ball to be taken up in unfamiliar hands. When William Shakespeare admonished Laertes in *Hamlet* (Act 1, Scene III), he spoke indirectly to all Scryers:

> *This above all: to thine own self be true,*
> *And it must follow, as the night the day,*
> *Thou canst not then be false to any man.*

When the crystal ball is not in use it should be placed on its pedestal in the center of the table. A black silk handkerchief is the perfect cover for it. The cover not only protects the globe from dust, but its more subtle purpose is to refute random reflections, which would disturb the rest periods of the crystal ball. Upon leaving the room, the scryer should further protect the crystal ball by locking the door.

How to Use the Crystal Ball

From the beginning of time, the one persistent question has been, "How does one make direct contact with the crystal ball?" Immediately three words present themselves—*belief*, *concentration*, and *patience*. All three are equally important; seership depends upon them. If an individual has an inborn ability to fix the mind or to concentrate, that person is well on the way to becoming a scryer.

However, none of the three will be as effective if the seer is not at ease physically. A posture chair will free the scryer from being distracted by seeking a more comfortable position.

Nothing is more vital than the breath, which is the source of all energy. It behooves every seer to learn to control the breath and to make it a habit. All professional seers, like all professional clairvoyants, cultivate deep breathing for they are aware their psychic powers are enhanced by their lung capacity. Deep breathing is a great aid to concentration, just as physical ease helps erase irritability, and assures a patient attitude.

The time factor enters strongly into gazing. There are three periods during the day that are ideal to consult the crystal ball— sunrise, midday, and sunset. It is generally accepted that sunrise is the most propitious, for it symbolizes a new beginning. This does not preclude other hours between dawn and dark.

There are definite times to avoid using the crystal ball. Those are the dark hours from nine o'clock in the evening until dawn. During that period the scryer is renewing vital powers, either through sleep or meditation.

If a person is inclined to mischievousness or even wickedness, it is necessary to warn that individual of the potential dangers of misusing the crystal ball. If the seer's purpose is to malign, eventually a disastrous and regrettable effect will be the outcome. This is not to infer that a seer must pose as a "goody-goody"—far from it. A scryer should be an even-tempered, intelligent, joyous, unselfish being. As was previously indicated, consistent use of the crystal ball has improved the health and augmented the vital powers.

Interpretation of Phenomena Seen in the Crystal Ball

Clouds

Generally, the first thing of which a novice becomes conscious is a clouding of the crystal ball. This clouding may appear in various forms: 1) as a milky obscurity, 2) as a smoky impenetrable mist, 3) as minuscule white clouds drifting through the crystal ball. *White clouds are an affirmative indication of coming favors.*

If a brilliance breaks through the clouds, it is indicative of the sun, which will light the way to better financial circumstances and to improved physical health. However, *if a soft light lacking brilliance appears* through the clouds, it is indicative of the moon, which foretells a period of inaction that may be likened to recuperating the vital forces.

When the cloud is black, that is the time to be concerned, for a black cloud is unfavorable, even ill-omened. The seriousness of the prediction is measured by the degree of blackness. Does the blackness appear in a small portion of the crystal ball, or does it fill the entire globe?

Occasionally, the clouds take on a show of color. If green, blue, or violet suffuse the crystal ball, this is an excellent indication. *When green clouds appear*, the individual will be called upon to assist as a neighborhood mediator in an educational, political, or religious capacity. *If a blue cloud appears*, an occasion will arise that requires shrewd discernment, which brings both honor and praise to the individual. *When a violet cloud floats through the crystal ball*, a latent talent may be recognized, or a worthy philosophical expression will be presented and well received.

When clouds of red, orange, or yellow appear the portents are ominous. *Red clouds foretell* dangerous situations—accidents, serious illness, and grief. *Orange clouds predict* loss of material goods as well as loss of friendships. *Yellow clouds bring* deception and ultimate betrayal by supposed friends.

Directions

Clouds that move upward in the crystal ball are positive signs. The questions may regard anything that is uppermost in the interrogator's mind; for example, business, health, housing, matrimony, social activities, or any of a myriad subjects.

Clouds that move downward in the crystal ball are negative. Every question earns a "no." However, it must be realized that it is the question itself that causes the cloud to appear and descend.

Clouds that move to the right of the seer announce the presence of spiritual beings. They are benign and ensure their willingness to assist both the seer and the individual seeking assistance.

Clouds that move to the left of the seer indicate a refusal to continue the "sitting" at that time. *Do not be discouraged!* Arrange another séance with the scryer in the near future.

Often it is necessary to look to far-distant places for a complete answer. Under such circumstances look into the crystal ball from a lengthwise angle. (Note: It may require practice on the part of the seer to learn to gaze lengthwise. It is well to practice before receiving a client.) Distance is not a determent to the crystal ball, for in its unfathomable depth reposes the whole of Creation.

The images that appear on the right hand of the seer are symbolic; for example, a ring may indicate an engagement; a briefcase may portend a business appointment; a flower may be interpreted in several ways according to the interests of a client, who may be interested in gardens, or may be considering marriage, or is celebrating a birthday. Symbols and their interpretations are endless.

The images that appear to the left of the scryer are the actual pictures of objects significant in the interrogator's life. Also, both the symbolic pictures and the factual pictures may assume the colors that appeared in the clouds and have a similar effect. For instance, if a reddish car appears, an accident may be imminent. However, if a green car should appear, its errand in all probability is for a good cause; for example, corresponding to the owner's position in life.

The Search for the Secret of Crystal Gazing

Some form of crystal gazing has been recognized since the ancients used ice for divination. As time passed and ice gave way to quartz, there was even more interest in the crystal ball. In the Middle

Ages elaborate rituals were invoked before the seer took up the crystal ball and prayerfully read the symbols that appeared, believing they had heavenly origin.

Naturally there is the skeptic who dismisses the whole thing with a shrug and claims it is due to the working of an immature mind that is too easily hoaxed. Fortunately, however, there is that rare individual with a thoroughly scientific attitude who endeavors to search for the truth and refuses to give credence to his own doubts. Such individuals in high places are now looking at the crystal ball with renewed interest.

Lewis Spence, one of the world's foremost scholars of occult science has this to say in his *An Encyclopedia of Occultism*, "The object of crystal gazing . . . is the induction of an hypnotic state giving rise to visionary hallucinations, the reflection of light in the crystal forming *points de repére* for such hallucinations." Later, he says, "There are many well-attested cases wherein the crystal has been successfully used for the purpose of tracing criminals, or recovering lost or stolen property."

While the present-day seer gives the crystal ball all the attention the long-ago scryer did, ritual has little place in the sittings. For instance, in the early seventies, the author was privileged to accompany a seer to an executive building in Westchester County, New York. Within a short time, three of the company's presidents had died, apparently of the same illness, which the attending physicians had found puzzling. The three men had occupied the same suite. The man selected to assume the presidency had qualms about accepting the position.

When the president-to-be recalled an acquaintance who was a respected seer, he hastily invited him to visit the building. Upon arrival it was noticeable that the grass outside the part of the building in question was brown and dying, and a young tree nearby was drooping and dropping leaves. With no preamble, the seer took from a pocket a small leather case, from which he lifted a magnificent, unblemished crystal ball the size of a child's marble. It was suspended from a ring of minuscule gold lilies. Almost immediately that beautiful clear crystal globe became a dull gray, as if a dark cloud passed through it. What appeared to be a small yellow stone became visible off left center. Quickly the seer demanded to be taken to the room that overlooked the yard where we stood. Eight paces from the window the yellow object deepened in color, and the gray cloud darkened. The seer said, "There is an underground stream here from which noxious vapors are rising. It should be a simple matter to correct this." Gently and carefully he returned the crystal ball to its velvet-lined box.

This proved true. After an excavation revealed the stream, and it was successfully diverted, the grass grew outside the window, the tree became healthy, and the newly appointed president remained in excellent health. However, the point is, *there was no ritual to invoke the crystal ball*. Obviously the seer had perfect rapport with his crystal, and he knew it.

Another extraordinary demonstration of crystal gazing, which is a proven fact, was the locating of the present Dalai Lama—the Fourteenth. Each Dalai Lama is the reincarnation of his predecessor. Recently the Thirteenth Dalai Lama had died and the immediate search for his reincarnation began. Undeniable evidence led to the belief that the child would be found in the East. This time the Crystal Ball was the picturesque Lake Lhamoi Latso at Chokhorgyal. (Note: According to John Melville, water has been used effectively in lieu of quartz.) The Tibetans believed that visions of the future may be seen in this beautiful lake, so the Regent journeyed ninety miles southeast to Chokhorgyal. He spent several days at Lake Lhamoi Latso in meditative prayer. Then the Regent saw the vision—a great monastery with green and gold roofs, and close by a dwelling with turquoise tiles. To the last detail the vision was correct, and the young boy who was destined to be the Dalai Lama was found living with his parents and siblings in the house with the turquoise tiles.

In this scientific age many attempts have been made to explain the appearance of clouds and pictures in the crystal ball. The question most often voiced is, "Is it possible for a Crystal Ball to pass through physical changes, especially if has been used for an extended period?" Andrew Lang, who wrote learnedly on crystal gazing, remarked especially on the "milky obscurity" that seemed to pervade the crystal ball. When he wrote about crystal gazing, W.R. Newbold also commented on the "milky masses." This led some to believe that self-hypnosis on the part of the scryer produced the manifestations, which were illusions. Immediately, this conclusion was discarded by dedicated seers.

However, our endeavor to solve an age-old problem begins with a demanding "W*hy*?" The seers have begun to look fearlessly and eagerly into the cause of the manifestations.

It is conceded that visible objects *are* moved by psychokinetic energy. There are numerous cases on record to verify this. Since it is an undeniable fact that psychokinetic energy moves visible objects, then it is feasible that invisible molecules may be manipulated by that same energy; for instance, regrouping atomistic objects to form patterns or pictures or to cloud the crystal ball according to the seer's concentrative power.

Still another question presents itself: "Why are the images in the crystal ball so ephemeral?" There is the possibility that as soon as the seer has received his answer, it becomes part of his store of knowledge and needs no further outward preservation. It may be likened to a problematic equation on a blackboard that has served its purpose. The blackboard is then cleared for the next example. So long as the seer concentrates, the molecules regroup themselves until the sitting is closed.

Crystallography, the science that deals with the system of configuration among crystals, their structure and forms of aggregation, verifies the resilence and cohesion in crystals. This geological evidence proves further that the images in the crystal ball are not illusions.

Once it has been acknowledged that psychokinetic energy affects matter, it follows that use of the mind's psychic force combined with the sensitive crystal ball is incalculable. The present-day scryer is in an enviable position. What individuals have done with the crystal ball while being unaware of the psychokinetic energy working through it, and while being unaware, also, of the efficiency of their marvelous brain power to direct it, is not to be compared with the promise of the future use of the crystal ball.

Dr. James Hyslop foresaw this Renaissance of crystal gazing when he said in his *Enigmas of Psychical Research* (1906): "The incidents in crystal vision apparently showing supernormal acquisition of knowledge so far transcend all that we ordinarily know of acute sensibility that we can only use this last fact (that the limits of knowledge are not confined by normal sensation and perception) as evidence of the possibility of much more besides, and prosecute our inquiries until we find a pathway into the deeper mysteries of the mind."

Part 2

Stones, Amulets, and Talismans for Power, Protection, and Prophecy

Witch Bree

1

The Transformational Power of Crystals

Humankind has been interested in stones, crystals, and gemstones for untold centuries. Primitive peoples probably picked up stones by impulse and out of curiosity. Through trial and error, they discovered which ones were more durable and fashioned them into tools that withstood the strain of hard use. Likewise, they noticed that some stones wore down more quickly while others could be polished to a lovely sheen.

The earliest humans also made use of the unique properties of crystals and used them for ceremonial decoration. Amber was possibly the first stone used for ornamentation. We have found ancient amber artifacts dating as far back as the Stone Age, showing that these early humans had discovered the rock-hard resin deposits that make amber and fashioned them into roughly rounded beads for necklaces, belts, and pouches. Archaeologists and anthropologists have found many sites in which precious amber was buried with the tools and remains of shamans, medicine men, and rulers. We can see that since these very early days, amber has been thought to have healing properties, a belief that stays with us to this day.

Obsidian was another early stone used for decoration, as we can see from deposits dating back to the Neolithic Age. Various gems such as lapis lazuli, amber, and pearls were made into powder and taken orally as medicine. And the first humans polished the shiny surface of jet and used it for mirrors to see not only the present but also the future.

The Egyptians were perhaps the first people most conscious of the power of crystals. They even placed them in the cornerstones of the Great Pyramids. They used gems as objects of protection, power, wisdom, and as symbols to show love for the living and the dead. A very important part of the Egyptian burial ritual made use of lapis lazuli, obsidian, turquoise, quartz, and carnelian. They carefully placed these stones inside the burial chamber. Each one had a specific purpose within the burial rite; for example, carnelian had the power to transport the souls of the dead to the other side. People traveled far and wide throughout the ancient world to obtain these precious, pretty rocks.

Today, people use gems and crystals as personal power tools to enhance their lives. Certain stones bring love into one's life. Others can heal the body and bring a sense of well-being. Still others create prosperity or aid in divining the future. By utilizing and integrating crystals in your own life, you will reap countless benefits.

Stone, Crystal, or Precious Gem?

Before we begin, it might be helpful to get some clarity on the terms "stone," "crystal," and "gemstone" or "gem." The broad category of "stones" actually includes the items in the other two categories, as it consists of all minerals that are crystalline in nature. It includes quartz crystals and diamonds, which are obviously crystalline in structure, as well as stones such as turquoise and agate that don't look like typical clear crystals because their crystalline form is not visible to the naked eye.

The terms "gemstone" and "gem" refer to stones that are made up of the same chemical compounds as the common variety of a mineral, but they are considered valuable because of their beauty, rarity, and clarity of color. For instance, a ruby is the gemstone form of the mineral red corundum, and an amethyst is a "semi-precious" type of quartz crystal.

So the terms "stones," "crystals," and "gems" all refer to crystalline substances, and I will use them interchangeably when I am speaking of crystals in general throughout the book. However, since each specific stone also has its own distinctive properties, I will refer to them separately by name as well, as we learn that these stones are not only lovely to look at and to adorn yourself with but also have powers that can bring you love, health, happiness, abundance, and peace of mind.

The Power of Crystals

Where do crystals get their power? They all have a crystalline structure that collects, stores, and releases electromagnetic energy in a manner that is similar to the way commonplace batteries store and release energy.

Scientists and engineers have discovered through experimentation that a crystal will accumulate and concentrate the energy of any given energy field in close proximity. Further, they've discovered that if a crystal is squeezed, energy from within the crystal is released. Light can also be released during the compression of a crystal. While the expansion is infinitesimal, electrons are emitted and are then reabsorbed by the crystal, thus producing energy. Schoolchildren discover this by rubbing or heating crystals and feeling a marked static charge. This is known as the piezoelectric effect. This effect can be quite powerful—it is one of the causes of earthquakes.

Quartz

Quartz is the largest of the crystal families, and we can be grateful for that since it is such a powerful healer. Quartz is also the crystal most often used today in both scientific and spiritual arenas. Quartz is, perhaps, the most common of all stones and can be found on virtually every landmass on Earth. Common quartz was used in the machinery that made the world's first radio broadcasts possible. It enabled the chips that propelled the computer revolution. It stands to reason that quartz was the first crystal to be synthesized by manufacture. Today, man-made crystals are used in many items including watches, computers, and other electronic devices.

Quartz is composed of silicon and oxygen, the same basic minerals that make up this planet. Silicon dioxide (SiO_2), the building block responsible for the geologic makeup of the earth, is also inside us, which may explain why there is a natural attraction between our bodies and crystals.

Quartz can take the form of great hexagonal stones or of crystals so small that only a microscope can see them. Quartz can appear in clusters or singly. It can also appear in every hue of the rainbow. The gorgeous and varied hues of quartz come from electrostatic energy, which now can be altered through technology. Most people, however, prefer the simple beauty provided by Mother Nature herself.

Thomas Edison carried quartz crystals with him at all times and called the stones his dream crystals. He believed they inspired his ideas and inventions. Literary legends George Sand and William Butler Yeats also relied on crystals to help spark their considerable creativity.

Data has also been gathered to show the effectiveness of quartz in certain healing techniques, such as chakra therapy, acupressure, and light-ray therapy, as we will discuss in depth later. Moreover, it functions as an energy regulator for the human body, affecting the vibrations of the *aura*, or energy field that surrounds all living beings. But the simplest way to promote healing with crystal is to wear a stone.

The Unique Qualities of Crystals

Crystals found in nature are imbued with special qualities from the minerals and rocks surrounding them. Geologists explain the varying colors of crystals in terms of chemical impurities. One way to think about crystalline color is similar to the way we think about what goes into making a fine wine, where the soil, neighboring trees, plants, sun, and rain affect the grapes and the resulting nectar. So, gems and crystals also have *notes*, like a fine wine. Truly gifted gemologists can distinguish these delicate differences, especially the vibratory distinctions from the slight variations in a crystal's structure and color.

We have a vast healing and life-enhancing trove of beautiful and sacred stones from which to choose, and each gem, crystal, and stone has its own inherent, divine qualities. Each stone is unique for the energy it emits and how it interacts with our subtle energy field, or aura. In the same way that no two fingerprints or snowflakes are alike, each crystal is completely unique, never to be repeated again in nature. Man-made crystals are exactly alike, and many people feel this uniformity reduces their appeal as well as their healing qualities.

Choosing Your Crystals

There are certain affinities between people and crystals that should be acknowledged. If you are attracted to a certain stone, by all means, investigate. Learn about the properties and characteristics of that particular gem or crystal and examine your present mental, emotional, or practical condition to see if you are in need of its properties. For instance, you may be attracted to striated quartz, which is a clear crystal embedded with needle-like streaks of gold. Gold is said to intensify the healing power of the quartz.

Striated quartz can carry more powerful healing properties and help cleanse your aura and awaken all your chakras, or energy centers (see Chakra Stones on page 47).

Citrine can help an individual hear and receive criticism gainfully. If you are attracted to citrine, consider carrying some with you and see if it opens you to reflection from others that can speed your personal development. So, please *do* listen to sudden stone attractions. Your body or subconscious may be sending you a very important message!

Included throughout this text and in the Crystal Lore section at the end are lists of stones and their affinities and healing properties. I encourage you to explore and discover those crystals that heal and energize you.

Let the Stones Speak

Part of the gem and crystal lore that has been developed over centuries is that of the power of special stones to give predictions or attract or repel certain energies. Here are a few examples of common attributes of specific stones:

- Agate worn as an amulet around your neck will ensure that you will speak only your truth. It can also attract favors from powerful people!

- Black agate on a short chain or in a ring will ensure success in business and athletic competition.

- Amazonite jewelry, worn while gambling, will bring good luck.

- Amber will attract love into your life and increase sensual pleasure if you wear it during lovemaking.

- Amethyst worn by a man will draw a good woman to him.

- Apache tear in a pendant will protect a woman in her pregnancy.

- Bloodstone jewelry worn in court helps bring victory in legal matters.

- Carnelian jewelry will keep you from being struck by lightning.

- Cat's-eye rings will retain your youthful beauty and lift depression.

- Coral earrings will attract men into your life. Pacific Islanders believe this "nature's jewel" contains the very essence of life.

- A diamond set in onyx will overcome sexual temptation and incite the loyalty of a partner.

- A diamond with a six-sided cut will offer you great protection. Set it in platinum and it will ensure victory in any conflict.

- Frog-shaped jewelry is the ultimate traveler's amulet; pilots, stewards, sailors, and anyone who frequently travels across water should wear frog-shaped aquamarine jewelry for enhanced safety and protection from drowning.

- Jade carved into the shape of a butterfly will attract love into your life.

- Jasper carved into the shape of an arrow will draw good luck to you.

- Lapis lazuli beads strung on gold wire will offer health, growth, and protection.

- Malachite gives great success to salespeople. Keep a malachite crystal in the cash register and wear it during trade shows, presentations, and meetings. If your malachite jewelry chips or breaks, beware! It is warning you of danger.

- Moonstone is the dieter's power stone and helps maintain youthful appearances and attitudes.

- Moss agate, worn while gardening, will bring a healthy harvest.

- Opal earrings will awaken your psychic powers.

- A red pearl ring or pendant will heighten intelligence.

- A dark peridot ring will bring you more money and raise your spirits, allaying melancholy or depression.

- Serpentine worn around a new mother's neck helps her flow of milk.

- A stone containing a fossil, such as amber, will lengthen your life span.

Working with Your Crystals

Once you've chosen a crystal, the first thing you need to do is to *charge* it, which means align it with your personal frequency and vibrations. You're placing your desires and wishes into the vessel of the crystal. The crystal's inherent energies will interact with your personal power, and your intentions can be manifested, or made real, through the crystal. Let's go through a step-by-step guide to align our crystals.

The very first step in this process is the dedication of the crystal toward the greater good of all beings. To begin, we must cleanse the crystal in order to purify its energy. Although this is a straightforward task, it is of supreme importance for your use of the crystal down the road. If a gem or stone is not as effective as you had hoped, the problem could stem from the initial dedication. Think of this primary step as the honing and direction of the intention.

Here is how to do it: Hold the crystal in the palm of your right hand and in your mind picture a glow of light surrounding it. When the stone is completely enveloped by light in your mind's eye, state out loud, "This crystal is only for exacting good of the highest order. In this stone of the earth, there is only love and light." Leave the crystal out in natural light of the sun and the moon for a twenty-four-hour period. This will give your crystal the maximum dedication of light and love from the universe and the heavens as part of its purification process.If time is of the essence, you can move right on to step number two, charging the crystal.

All stones possess natural energies of their own. You want to merge your energies with those of your crystals so that the crystals will be in sync with your vibratory channel or your essential body and spirit energy. Remain mindful of the power your stones have and you will be in a good position to work with them. Consider carefully what kind of energy you want to place into your crystal. Sit in a comfortable position and hold the crystal in your right hand. Focus on the energy you desire your crystal to hold and project it into the stone. Bear in mind, gem magic should not be used solely for your purposes, but always for the greater good. Please make sure you're projecting positive energy and not anger or hatred. Ask aloud for your crystal to work together with you for the highest good. You are doing creative visualization here, so keep concentrating until you can see and feel the energy flowing into the stone. You will feel when the charging is complete because your intuition will tell you when your crystal has stored enough energy.

You can charge a stone for someone else, although it is not ideal. For example, if you have a friend who is very ill and lives halfway around the world from you, you can charge the crystal with positive, healing energy and send it to your friend to help him. Ask the crystal to work for the highest good of this person and then release that crystal to him.

Crystal Care and Cleaning

After the first thirty-three days of tuning in with a new crystal, you should give it a good cleaning, both physically and energetically. Thirty-three is a power number and is the amount of time you need to wait for your crystal to be permeated with your personal psychic energy. I recommend keeping your crystal with you during this time—in a pocket or, if it is small, in a little pouch around your neck. The constant interaction with your body will get your crystal in sync with you.

There are many ways to clean your crystals. The simplest is to wash the crystal in warm water and then wipe it with a soft, natural-fabric cloth. Scott Cunningham, the esteemed author and expert on many magical matters, recommended that you utilize the power of moonlight—especially the strong light of the full moon—to cleanse and charge the crystal with your intentions. I cleanse my crystal before and after each use with rainwater that has sat through at least one day of sunlight and one night of moonlight. You can create your own cleansing rituals, adding ceremonial actions of your own or taking some from crystal lore. Your crystal rituals can get as elaborate as you want! To thoroughly cleanse your crystal, put it in a bowl of sea salt for seven days.

Your crystal is meant to be in harmony with your energy. Do not allow anyone else to touch your crystals. If by chance it happens, use one of the above methods to cleanse them of outside energy and influence.

Treat your crystals as the precious things they are. Keep them in a soft cloth; I prefer a dark blue silk bag. Never store your crystals in a synthetic material—they came from the earth and need to stay connected to the earth's grounding energy. Cunningham recommended wrapping your crystals in a soft white, yellow, or black cloth. Regard your crystals with the highest respect, and the highest mind, and they will give you a lifetime of service. Also, remember to remain mindful of how you are using them, and always only call on your crystals to assist you for the purposes of universal love and healing. If you do, the effects will be positive.

2

Crystal Tools for Protection, Prophecy, and Healing

The possibilities for applying crystal power in your life are truly limitless when you begin tapping in to the wisdom of the stones and using them as tools for prophecy, protection, and healing. You can purchase ready-made tools or fashion your own ritual accessories from crystals you find yourself. Your intentions and personal energy are the driving forces behind the enchantments you create. You'll be amazed as the various crystal accoutrements start to collect and hold the energy of your magical workings. You may start to experience how your power and your care for the greater good grows.

Prophecy Stones

Healers, shamans, witch doctors, and medicine men have been using special stones—the bones of the earth—for divination since time immemorial. Lore around stones has developed in different cultures. In Europe, during the Middle Ages and the Renaissance, crystals became widely used as tools to help predict the future. The desert civilizations of the Middle East called crystals "prophecy stones," and ancient Egyptians believed that holding such a crystal gave one access to the Akashic Record, or the great storehouse containing all the knowledge accumulated throughout time.

Scrying

There is no future to look into, there is only the Great Now.
Lon Milo DuQuette

It seems that everyone wants to see into the future, and scrying is an ancient method of doing exactly that. Scrying is the art of divining by gazing at or into an appropriate surface and receiving information about the future in the form of visions. The reflective surface could be water, a mirror, a crystal ball, or a slab of stone. Some people are quite talented at seeing visions in the flames of fire or in the bottom of a teacup. However, smooth, neutral surfaces are much less distracting.

We don't know how the art of scrying first began. Perhaps a chunk of shiny black obsidian was the first scrying mirror. We do know that ancient civilizations had special prophets and priestesses who engaged in foretelling the future. They made the tools of their trade from various crystals they found in their locale. No doubt these ancient future-seers would be delighted to know we are still using crystal balls made from translucent quartz and mysterious volcanic obsidian, the same materials they used!

Scrying is even mentioned in Genesis 44:4–5. Queen Elizabeth I entrusted all matters of the heavens and the future to John Dee, a brilliant mathematician and metaphysician. Dee used a mirror of polished black obsidian and employed scrying to great effect in calling upon certain angels. He reported hearing knocking and even voices that sounded like an owl screeching during sessions. His skill and legacy led succeeding magicians and psychics to prefer black mirrors.

Scrying can be also be used to divine the past, present, and future. You can contact spirit guides, improve your skills of creative visualization, and even use it as a gateway to the astral plane.

Any time you feel the need for insight and answers, scrying can lend illumination. Are you stymied at work? Are you restless and don't know why? Do you suspect someone isn't being honest with you? Try scrying!

Crystal Balls

Highly polished, glasslike spheres of beryl and quartz crystal have been in use for thousands of years. Biblical priests used shewstones, as crystal balls were known in those times, to communicate with higher beings and divine the future. Abbot Tritheim, who taught the 15th-century German mystic and alchemist Cornelius Agrippa von Nettesheim, had very specific guidelines for the size and color of crystal balls. He recommended they be "the bigness of a small orange," and also of complete and absolute clarity. Further, he urged diviners to mount their stone on a pedestal engraved with the "tetragrammaton," or the holy four-lettered name of god, YHVH, along with the names of Michael, Gabriel, Uriel, and Raphael, the four archangelic rulers of the Sun, Moon, Venus, and Mercury.

Great figures throughout the ages have recommended crystal balls to help look into the future or gain clarity on present situations. The great philosopher and physician Paracelsus declared during the height of the Renaissance that what he called "conjuring crystals" should be used in "observing everything rightly, earning and understanding what was." The scepter used by Scottish royalty contains a crystal ball, the usage of which was thought to have come down from the Druids. Another Scottish association is that of the "cairngorm," a large sphere of smoky quartz now housed in the British Museum, believed to be Sir John Dee's own crystal ball.

Sir Walter Scott referred to crystal balls as "stones of power."

In Asia, some of the finest crystal balls are the result of many years of patient hand polishing. For the Japanese, the "tama" is a crystal ball held to be the symbol of eternity.

The value of crystal balls shows up in our culture and collective mind-set. They can be found in mythic history: Merlin, the fabled wizard of Arthurian legend, was believed to have kept his crystal ball with him at all times. They can also be found in fairy tales, Disney stories, and even today's movies: the "palantirs" favored by the wizards in *The Lord of the Rings* were super-powered crystal balls.

Choosing a Crystal Ball

Choosing a crystal ball should not be undertaken lightly. They are a deeply personal tool and have their own energy. As you use them, they will also become imbued with your energy. Think of a crystal ball as a container for a great deal of your energy and make sure the one you choose feels right for you. It should have the right heft in your hand and feel comfortable as you hold and use it.

Pure quartz crystal balls can be costly, ranging from $1000 to $10,000 for a large crystal of excellent quality. A ball of that quality is well worth the expense if you are serious about harnessing your intuition and using it for good. Of course, you can find less expensive crystal balls that, through your concentration and focus, can also serve your purposes. Every crystal ball is unique and has its own energy. Crystal balls hewn from different materials also are said to enhance specific outcomes. Here are a few examples of stones and their properties:

- Amethyst opens your own psychic abilities and offers advice on business matters. It is especially good for lawyers and writers.
- Azurite with malachite helps with concentration and creativity when you are studying or brainstorming new ideas.

- Beryl helps you find anything you have lost—
  keys, jewelry, money, people!
- Bloodstone guards you against people who may be trying
  to deceive you.
- Celestite gives you the very special help of angel-
  powered insight and advice.
- Chrysocolla helps you to see and resolve relationship
  difficulties.
- Lapis lazuli leads the way if you are looking for a new job.
- Obsidian helps you see and resolve past-life issues.
- Quartz crystal can put you in touch with helpful spirit
  guides who foretell events.
- Selenite is particularly useful with any matters regarding
  hearth and home. Use selenite in the moonlight for
  pleasant visions of your future.
- Smoky quartz connects you with nature spirits and shows
  you what to avoid in your life.

Using Your Crystal Ball

Crystal balls have their own authority and wield a large influence
on the development of our psychic abilities. When you gaze into
a crystal ball, it is possible to see into the fabric of time, both the
past and the future. What you see could be a delineated vision
or a flickering, wispy suggestion of images. Most people who use
crystal balls, including many healers and teachers, see cloudy
and smoky images, so do not expect your experience to be like
going to the movies.

You have to practice and hone your attunement with the
energy of the crystal ball. Many psychics use crystal balls in their
readings, and some report seeing images of their clients' auras in
the ball. You have to get really clear on how you interpret what you
see. Divining information about other people's lives is a huge

responsibility, and you need to be sure what you are reading and that your perception will help them in a positive way. One way is to learn to find the center of intuition in your body. For me (and for many other people) this center is a gut feeling—literally in my stomach. I get a feeling of surety, of knowing. If I don't get any such bodily sensation, I simply explain that I don't know what I'm reading or I'm not really "getting anything." It is far better to say you don't know than to fake it or say something that could, even inadvertently, have a negative effect.

You can sharpen your psychic skills by working with a partner. Sit directly across from your partner with a crystal ball between you. Close your eyes halfway and look *at* the ball and *into* the ball while harnessing your entire mind. Empty out all other thoughts and focus as hard as you can. Your third eye—the chakra, or energy center located between your eyebrows—should begin to open, and the vision and intuition will come from there and project into the crystal ball. As you train your mind, the patterns will become clearer and your impressions will become surer. You should trust that what you are seeing is real and find a place of knowing, as I do in my stomach. Express to your partner what you are seeing. Then listen to your partner as she reveals her visions to you. After at least three rounds of individual reading and revealing, share visions at the same time and learn whether you are seeing the same things!

A mental practice to try on your own is this crystal-ball meditation: In a darkened room, sit holding your crystal ball in the palms of both of your hands. Touch it to your heart and then gently touch it to your forehead where the third eye resides. Then hold the ball in front of your eyes and, sitting very still, gaze into it for at least three minutes. Envision pure white light in the ball and hold that image. Practice the white-light visualization for up to a half hour and then rest your mind, your eyes, and your crystal ball. If you do this every day, within a month you will start to become adept at crystal-ball gazing.

Crystal Gazing

Nowadays, crystal balls can be extravagantly expensive. If you find that is the case when you begin looking, you can use other crystals as substitutes as a way to divine meaning. Any well-polished stone or crystal that has rainbow glints of color and various structures or features inside can also be a tool for prophecy. Find a stone that interests you and hold it in your hand. Now, close your eyes and clear other thoughts from your mind. When you have a sense of mental clarity and focus, open your eyes and begin gazing into your crystal. While you are focusing on the stone, allow the internal shapes and colors to flow into your mind. Images, impressions, and meaning will begin to take shape. When you feel ready, write down your impressions and reflect upon them. Go back a few days later, and you may be surprised at how much you gleaned from your crystal-gazing exercise. Continue this for a while and you will begin to see patterns of information about your present and future begin to emerge.

Another method of crystal divination using polished crystals and internally variegated quartzes is to look deeply within the crystal and visualize yourself *inside* the stone. Joules and Ken Taylor in their marvelous book *Clairvoyance: How to Develop Your Psychic Powers* suggest using a microscope so you can see the internal structures and striations as closely as possible. As they explain, "under a microscope, the internal structures of crystals resemble mazes, labyrinths, curves, spires, light-filled halls. Imagine what it would be like to wander through these features, exploring the crystal from the inside."

Crystals of Clairvoyance

These special stones assist psychic development:

- Azurite helps with the development of divination skills.

- Chaorite helps with spiritual development.

- Citrine is good for psychic awareness.

- Emerald dispels confusion.

- Peridot will ward off the energy of others.

- Rhodonite protects extra-sensitive people.

Stone Pendulums—Dowsing and Divining

The pendulum is a tool for gleaning information about your inner self. Some of the best pendulums are the ones you make yourself by tying a piece of string or rawhide to a crystal. You should tie it so that the crystal points down. Each time you use it, ask the pendulum to show you "yes." Whatever way the pendulum moves at that point—swinging side to side or up and down, or circling to the right or left—is your "yes." Do the same thing for a "no." Try keeping a journal of your work with the pendulum. Not only will this give you a record of the yes and no responses, but it will also help you track their effectiveness. You will learn so much about yourself and your place in the world. Some dowsers absolutely depend on their pendulums for help with all manner of decision-making.

Most metaphysical shops now sell lovely chunks of amethyst and quartz attached to delicate chains. Do try this easiest of all forms of divination. It is fun and full of surprising truths.

Rune Stones

Runes are symbolic letters derived from ancient English, Scandinavian, and German alphabets. When these letters are carved into stones and used to divine the future, their meanings are said to hone and intensify the intuition of the reader. Moonstone is reputed to be the most powerful crystal for use in rune stones. You, too, can use a bag of lustrous and mysterious moonstone runes to get in touch with your powers of perception. While others throw the I Ching or read their horoscopes with their morning coffee, you can pull a rune from the set you have either purchased or created yourself and contemplate its meaning for your day.

The Mystery of Mirrors

Mirrors are central tools of magicians. Shiny, smooth reflective surfaces lend themselves so well to the imagination and intuition. They act like portals to another world, promoting psychic awareness. Gazing balls and pools have also served for dealing with the divine.

Throughout history, people looking for answers have used mirrors and even bowls filled with ink to peer into another dimension. Obsidian and other types of shimmering rocks and volcanic glass were used by primitive peoples to communicate with unseen spirits, which is what we modern folk do when we are accessing energy. When Harry Potter famously looked into his magic mirror, he awakened the modern masses to this tradition. It was so compelling, sales of magic mirrors have skyrocketed.

You can make your own magic mirror and power it with crystals. First, get a round mirror, preferably with a plastic or wooden frame. This will make it easier to glue appliqués. Make sure the frame has a lot of surface area on which to affix your gems. From any New Age store or rock shop, purchase fifty to one hundred small crystals. Choose various quartzes and semiprecious stones of a similar shape and small size. Select a rainbow of colors or a single hue if you are feeling a particular affinity for a certain stone. Clean the frame with a soft, dry cloth and spread clear-drying glue onto it. One at a time, place the crystal pebbles on the frame in any pattern you desire. Make lovely versions of concentric colored circles following the rainbow spectrum. Begin with deepest, darkest red garnet stones inside and circle out to the palest purple pebbles and finally end with a layer of the clearest quartz.

I know some gem magicians who have several magic mirrors for different kinds of questing and querying. A mirror of peridot, the birthstone of Leo, is good for looking at issues of self-image. A ruby mirror, made of the highly affordable rough rubies, is perfect for matters relating to love, and a jade mirror will aid in money matters. If your astrological sign is one of the water signs (Cancer, Scorpio, and Pisces), you would do well to make magic mirrors from sea glass and seashells you have gathered during walks on the beach. Anyone who feels drawn to the ocean will also benefit from a seashell magic mirror. Many of us go for walks on the beach or along water when we are searching for answers. A magic mirror of shells can be twice as effective at helping you find your answers!

Amethyst is still one of the most available, most affordable, and most generally helpful of all crystals. A mirror adorned with amethyst is a very dependable tool of magic. Amethyst is a good balancing stone and is also one of the most intuition boosting of all gems.

A Stone's Throw Divination

Give your tarot cards a rest and create a one-of-a-kind divination tool, a bag of crystals. It is very easy to do. Take a favorite drawstring bag and fill it with the crystals listed in the guide below. Then when the need arises, turn to crystal visions for guidance. It is as easy as one, two, three: 1) shake the bag well, 2) ask a question, and 3) remove the first three stones you touch and interpret them using the guide.

If you are like most folks, you *cannot* afford diamonds in your bag of tricks, so substitute with clear quartz; for emeralds, include peridot. Garnets exchange nicely for rubies. I was happy to note that the marvelous metaphysical store Magus in Minneapolis has a lovely crystal ball and stone collection for sale (1-800-99MAGUS or www.magusbooks.com) and even had rough-ruby and rough-emerald pieces at $3 each, so the real deal is becoming more readily available all the time. The following stones can be used in divination bags to indicate these messages:

- Agate: Business success and notoriety are near.
- Amethyst: Change is coming.
- Aventurine: New horizons and positive growth are ahead.
- Black agate: Monetary gain is certain.
- Blue lace agate: There's a need for spiritual and physical healing.
- Citrine: The universe offers enlightenment.
- Diamond: Stability is sure.
- Emerald: Look for total abundance.
- Hematite: Examine new prospects.
- Jade: Expect to live a long life.
- Lapis lazuli: Harness heavenly fortune.
- Quartz: Receive clarity where there was none.
- Red agate: Expect long life and health.
- Red jasper: Notice the need for grounding.
- Rose quartz: Love is in your life.
- Ruby: Dare for deep passion and personal power.
- Sapphire: Time for truth.
- Snowflake obsidian: Your troubles are at an end.
- Snow quartz: Make major changes.
- Tiger's-eye: The situation is not as it appears.

Tools and Talismans for Power and Protection

Crystals can be catalysts for positive change and tools you can consciously use to protect yourself and bring love, prosperity, and health into your life. By buying or crafting crystal wands, amulets, and talismans for yourself or loved ones, you can harness the power of the stones—and of Earth itself—for your own positive purposes.

Wielding Wands

The most important tool for many people is the wand. Wands are used to focus your intention in spells and magical ceremonies. There are many gorgeous, crystal-encrusted wands for sale in metaphysical shops, doubtless quite effective in their own way. Bear in mind, though, that it is a wonderful thing indeed to make your own wand. Start with a tree branch that has fallen to the ground on its own. Sand and polish the rough edges, as it is a wand and not a weapon. Then give it a good smudging by passing it through smoke from burning sage. Attach a large quartz crystal onto the wand near the handle, and attach any crystals featuring properties that will complement your magic. Citrine makes an excellent pointer tip for your wand and aligns your self-identity with your spirit.

These stones are highly recommended as catalysts to help you harness specific powers. Attach these stones to your wand; you can change and experiment with the stones you use to enhance different properties and strengthen different characteristics:

- Amber for grounding
- Amethyst for balance and intuition
- Aventurine for creative visualization
- Bloodstone for abundance and prosperity
- Calcite for warding off negativity

- Carnelian for opening doors and helping you overcome any family problems
- Chalcedony for power over dark spirits
- Citrine for getting motivated and attracting money and success
- Fluorite for communicating with fairies and other unseen beings
- Garnet for protection from gossip
- Geode for getting through periods of extreme difficulty,
- Hematite for strength and courage
- Jade for wisdom or to realize powerful dreams
- Jasper for stability
- Lodestone for bringing a lover back into your life
- Mahogany obsidian for feeling sexy and emanating sensuality
- Moss agate for powers of persuasion and healing
- Quartz crystal for divining night dreams
- Rhodochrosite for staying on course with your life's true purpose
- Rose quartz for love
- Turquoise for safety when traveling
- Watermelon tourmaline for help planning your best possible future

Amulets

An amulet is a charm inscribed with a symbol or incantation that protects the wearer from evil or disease. The use of amulets dates from the earliest human beliefs. The peoples of the Mesopotamian plain wore them. The Assyrians and Babylonians favored cylindrical seals encrusted with precious stones. They also loved animal talismans and associated them with the qualities of the different animals: lions for courage, bulls for virility, and so on. The ancient Egyptians depended on their amulets for use in burial displays, and we can see many preserved in the cases of today's museums. To make their amulets, the Egyptians employed a material called faience, a glazed composition of ground quartz that was typically blue green in color. Wealthier denizens of the Nile, royalty, and the priestly class wore precious and semiprecious gems and crystals as amulets. Lapis lazuli was perhaps the most revered of these and was worn in many shapes, the eye of Horus being the most significant religious icon, followed by the scarab, symbolizing rebirth; the frog, symbolizing fertility; and the ankh, representing eternal life.

Pliny the Elder, the Roman philosopher and scientist who wrote *Naturalis Historia* in A.D. 77, subscribed to the use of amulets and wrote about three common kinds used by the Romans of the classical age. A typical amulet of that era was a bit of parchment inscribed with protective words, rolled up in a metal cylinder, and worn around the neck. Evil eyes were the most common of all amulets, the belief being that they could ward off a hex by simply reflecting it back to its origins. Phallic symbols have always been popular, too, coming in the shapes of horns, hands, and the phallus, of course. Some amulets were devoted to a specific god or goddess, providing protection by that particular entity to the wearer of such a piece.

Organized religions appropriated the idea of amulets from pagan peoples. It was very popular in medieval times for Jews, Christians, and Muslims to wear a tiny verse from the Torah, the Bible, or the Koran, respectively. Today, many Catholics wear a medal honoring a given saint, such as Saint Christopher, the patron saint for travelers. Wiccans and modern pagans are great proponents of protective amulets, causing resurgence in fascination with Celtic symbols and imagery.

Amulets are very easy to create and make nice gifts, as long as you believe your friends will truly benefit from them and are aware of the special qualities and powers they hold. To make one, select a crystal that is endowed with the desired energy. Hold it in the palm of your hand until it is warm from your touch. Then, visualize the specific power the stone is offering. If you're giving your amulet to yourself, wear it as a pendant or tuck it into your pocket or purse as a "guardian to go." Here is a list of stones and their qualities so you can choose a specific safeguard appropriate to your needs:

- Amethyst helps with sobriety by preventing inebriation.
- Aquamarine is good for attracting wisdom and overcoming a fear of water and drowning. It is also a guard against malevolent spirits.
- Bloodstone brings luck and is good to wear during travels.
- Carnelian is to the devil as garlic is to a vampire—keeps him away!
- Chrysolite drives away evil spirits and promotes peaceful sleep, especially if set in gold.
- Diamond in a necklace brings good fortune and lends force and valor. This dazzling stone should always touch the skin and works best when it is received as a gift.
- Emerald can cancel out the power of any magician!
- Jade offers protection, especially for children, and guards their health. It also creates prosperity.
- Jasper is reputed to be a defense against the venom of poisonous insects and snakes.
- Jet set in silver will help expel negativity.
- Moonstone is another boon to travelers and also brings fortune and fame.
- Turquoise is believed to be great for a horse's gait if affixed to the animal's bridle.

Talismans

A talisman is a decorative object that also provides protection and has magical properties. The reasons for using talismans are many—for love, for wealth, for luck with gambling, for the gift of a silver tongue, for a good memory, for the prevention of death. Whatever you can think of, there is probably a talisman for that exact purpose!

People often confuse amulets with talismans, but they differ in this significant way: Amulets *passively protect* the wearer from harm, evil, and negativity. Talismans *actively transform* the wearer and give the wearer certain powers. For example, the supernatural sword Excalibur, imbued with supremacy by the Lady of the Lake, gave King Arthur magical powers.

Grimoires (spell books) offer instruction on making talismans. But a talisman can be any article or symbol that you believe has mystical qualities. As we know, many gems and crystals have special innate powers. With a talisman, the special powers can be naturally present or instilled during a ritual.

Sacred Stone Shapes

- Ankh-shaped stones represent the key to life. This ancient Egyptian symbol can bring creativity, wisdom, and fertility.

- Clusters are among the most common natural crystal forms and bring balance and harmony into your life.

- Diamond-shaped stones bring the energy of wealth and abundance and are said to attract riches.

- Egg-shaped stones denote creativity and give new ideas to those who wear them.

- Heart-shaped stones are love energy. They promote self-love and romance.

- Holes that form naturally in stones are very auspicious and magical. If you look through the holes by the light of the moon, you can see visions and spirits.

- Human body–shaped stones bring good energy and strengthen the body parts depicted.

- Obelisks are four-sided, pyramid-topped shapes and are wonderful energy activators, or manifesters. Write your wish down on paper and place it beneath an obelisk to bring that hope into reality.

- Octahedrons, eight-sided stones, bring order to chaos and are great for analysis and organization. They are also terrific for healing. Carry an octahedron crystal in your pocket if you are unwell, so you will feel better soon.

- Pyramid-shaped stones carry energy upward, toward their pointed tips. I have a beautiful little malachite pyramid that I keep on my computer simply because I love to look at it. When the need arises, however, I can place a dollar bill underneath it and visualize positive money energy flowing up out of the stone, and abundance always follows.

- Rectangular rocks and crystals represent the energy of God. In addition to symbolizing male energy and the phallus, this shape is symbolic of energy itself and electrical current. It also denotes protection. Rectangular stones are great for love and sex spells.

- Round stones represent the universe and the Goddess. They are symbols of spirituality, connection to the universe, femininity, and, of course, pregnancy. Round crystals can be used in all love spells to cause attraction.

- Square stones represent the earth and are harbingers of plenty and prosperity.

- Triangular stones are guardian stones and protect the wearers.

The Healing Power of Crystals

One of the primary reasons crystals populate our planet is for healing. Currently, there is an upsurge in the healing power of crystals and an extensive array of curative crystals. However, do not ever replace traditional medicine with a crystal-only approach. A combination of Eastern and Western medicine, inclusive of gem and crystal healing, is the best way to cover all of your bases for health and wellness. Gem healing can be the difference between feeling okay and feeling GREAT. And, who wouldn't want to feel wonderful?

Repairing Your Aura with Crystals

We have all encountered psychic vampires, whether we know it or not. The problem is your aura will know it because psychic vampires tear away little pieces of your *chi*, or life force, leaving holes in your aura. You can identify the places that need patching because they will become noticeably cold as you pass a crystal over them. Pick your favorite stone from amethyst, citrine, or quartz and run it all around you at a distance of about three inches. Make note of the cold spots and lay the crystal on those places for up to five minutes, until the spot feels warmer. You will have repaired the holes in your etheric body, or aura, and should begin to feel a pleasant sense of renewed wholeness once again.

Here's another technique to try: crystal combing. It sounds odd, but you will become an aficionado immediately after you have felt the wonderfully soothing results. The beautiful pink kunzite is amazing as a mental-management crystal. Take the crystal and brush it in gentle, slow, downward strokes from the top of your head, the crown chakra, to the bottom of your feet. The next time you feel overwhelmed by anxiety, try this and you will feel more relaxed and in control afterward.

Kunzite is also a heart mender, touch it on the heart chakra to bring inner peace, clear away old romantic wounds, and get rid of emotional baggage. You can place a chunk of kunzite upon your chest, meditate with it, and feel the healing energy flow in.

Cranium-Calming Crystals

The main causes of headaches are stress, anxiety, and negative responses to various foods. Lapis lazuli has been used to treat headaches for millennia. Amethyst and turquoise are also good stones. Often stomach unrest can signal the brain to have a headache, and stones such as citrine and moonstone can create a calm that soothes the stomach and staves off a related headache.

Pain-Relief Prisms

Crystals have very mild and serene ways of tranquilizing negative energy and releasing pain. Ever so gently rub the crystal across the inflamed area. The stone will feel cool and calming. Visualize the pain going into the crystal, and the crystal forming a prism that contains the pain. Carnelian works well and is also meant to be particularly effective for helping bones to heal, but quartz can also serve the purpose. Place rose quartz, turquoise, or carnelian over the heart area, the solar plexus, and as the crystal touches upon the heart chakra, feel the fear dissolving while the pain gradually lessens.

Copper is unmatched for dealing with edema, the swelling and inflammation that can be caused by arthritis, repetitive stress injuries, sports-related soreness, and many other issues. Malachite can be a great agent for pain reduction. It has a lot of the mineral copper in it. Try wearing a malachite pendant, ring, or bracelet. Iron-rich magnetite is another pain absorber.

Laying On of Stones

This crystal-healing practice is distilled from the study of chakras. Here are just a few examples of how to apply crystals directly upon your body or that of anyone else who needs healing. The first step for anyone undertaking crystal healing is to lie down, relax, and get very comfortable. Empty everything else from your mind.

Lapis lazuli and its blue aquamarine can be laid upon the throat chakra to release any blockage therein. This greatly aids in self-expression and is wonderful for professional speakers as well as performers such as actors and singers. Turquoise laid on the face—cheeks, forehead, and chin—is a calming agent, significantly reducing tension. Azurite on the brow opens the third eye and deepens wisdom; this can be a door opening to enlightenment.

Clear quartz crystal placed upon the brow, each cheek, and the chin can balance the energy of the head and allow more light into the third eye.

Malachite, a heart stone, placed near the heart and along the center of the abdomen will create a sense of harmony and facilitate letting go of pain, suffering, and old childhood wounds.

The Rainbow is a simple and effective method for total-body wellness. Choose from this list of stones, making sure you have one of each color of the rainbow—violet, indigo, blue, green, yellow, orange, and red—plus one white stone and one black stone for completion. Then, simply lay the stones on their corresponding chakra centers. Following is a list of crystal and body affinities in case there is any specific area you want to focus on.

- Appendix: Chrysolite
- Bladder: Orange calcite
- Blood and circulatory system: Hematite
- Bone marrow: Purple fluorite
- Eyes: Beryl
- Feet: Smoky quartz
- Hands: Moldavite
- Heart: Rose quartz
- Intestines: Celestite
- Joints: Magnetite
- Kidneys: Bloodstone

- Knees: Jadeite
- Liver: Carnelian
- Lungs: Dioptase
- Male vitality: Topaz
- Muscles: Danburite
- Nervous system: Dendrite agate
- Pancreas: Chrysocolla
- Pituitary: Benitoite
- Prostate: Chrysoprase
- Shins and skin: Brown jasper
- Skeletal system: Calcite
- Spine: Garnet
- Spleen: Chalcedony
- Stomach: Fire agate
- Teeth: Fluorite
- Throat: Lapis lazuli
- Thymus: Blue tourmaline
- Thyroid: Amber
- Womb area: Moonstone

Chakra Stones

The concept of chakras originated many thousands of years ago in Asia. The ancient philosophers and metaphysicians identified seven main energy centers in the body and saw each chakra emanating energy in the form of a rainbow color that affected the mental, physical, and spiritual balance in a human being. The chakras are named in descending order in accordance with their placement in the body: crown, brow, throat, heart, solar plexis, sacral, and root.

Chakra theory is the basis of many Eastern healing practices. One of the simplest ways to achieve well-being is to place crystals on the parts of the body where certain chakras are centered. Many people credit their clarity and well-being to chakra therapy.

Following is a table showing corresponding relationship between each chakra and its associated color, energy, and crystal.

Chakra	Color	Energies	Corresponding Crystals
First—Root (base of spine)	Red	Security, Survival	Garnet, Smoky quartz
Second—Sacral	Orange	Pleasure	Amber, Carnelian
Third—Solar plexus	Yellow	Drive, Personal power	Amber, Citrine, Topaz
Fourth—Heart	Green	Abundance, Love, Serenity	Peridot, Rose quartz
Fifth—Throat	Blue	Creativity, Originality	Blue quartz, Tiger's-eye
Sixth—Third eye	Indigo	Intuitiveness, Perception	Fluorite, Lapis lazuli
Seventh—Crown	Violet	Holy bliss; All is one	Amethyst, Diamond

Colors and Shapes—Crossing the Rainbow Bridge

The colors of stones, gems, and minerals have great meaning and are clues to the power that lies within the crystalline structures. Color is one form of energy with individual vibrations. It is becoming common knowledge that the color in our work and home environments can affect our moods, calm us down, make us more energetic or romantic, and promote any number of desired states of being.

The color system springs from seven basic vibrations, the same ones at the foundation of our chakra system and also of the musical scale. The "heaviest" vibrations are at the bottom, and the "lightest" vibrations are at the top. Each of the seven basic colors relates to one of the seven chakras. Highly skilled psychics can read your aura and see the energy radiating out from your body as colors. You can use color management on the simplest level each day of your life. If you wake up feeling depressed, wear yellow to raise your energy level. If you are having a big business meeting, wear red, the power color. If you have a meeting and you want to put your colleagues at ease, wear brown or green, the earth colors, and you will see them relax. When you need inspiration, wear blue, and, finally, wear purple when you want to be at your most spiritual.

Following is a guide to colors. Don't be afraid to let go and work with a multitude of hues. Have fun, and remember how you feel while you are learning and experimenting!

Red

Red relates to the root chakra and corresponds to security and survival issues. On an emotional level, red is passion and intensity. On a healing level, it is warmth and fights cancer.

Subcolors of red are rose red, deep red, and orange red. Rose red corresponds to issues concerning one's mother, home, grounding, and money; emotionally, rose red corresponds to love. Deep red corresponds to the sense of smell; emotionally, it indicates anger. Orange red corresponds to sexual passion.

Red is the most physical of the colors and is also a strong emotional color. Red gems and crystals are the ones that will aid you in matters of the body. Jasper, amber, and agate in shades of red can help shy people feel stronger. I am seeing a huge resurgence of interest in red coral. This stone is a great help to the skeleton and bones. Nowadays, people need to feel their vitality more than ever. Red coral is also a boost to the lungs. There has been an increase in influenza, tuberculosis, and asthma such as we have not seen since the Depression era. Red coral may be able to help your health.

For the Chinese, red rice symbolizes immortality. In the tarot, the Hermit, the High Priestess, and the Empress wear red beneath blue robes, symbolizing the great hidden knowledge they hold. Dark red relates to female mysteries and the source of all life.

Pink is a sweeter color and has a calmer vibration than the reds. Where red is passionate, pink is nurturing. Pink is the esteem-

boosting color and can direct love to the self, which is very important in this day and age when people are so directed by others.
Pink pearl will also make your intuition about love and romance
more accurate. Those of us who tend to pick the wrong people in
love matters could do well to sport a pink pearl ring or pendant.
Pink coral makes for a sweet, upbeat, and more genuinely loving
attitude. Rose quartz will help in self-enhancement and direct-
ing positive energy toward the self. Rhodonite, rhodochrosite, or
a big pink diamond will help build an unconditionally positive
regard within and without.

Orange

Orange relates to the sacral chakra, or abdominal region, and
corresponds to physical urges such as hunger and sex.
Emotionally, it corresponds to ambition. It helps heal sexual
issues, increases potency, and builds stronger immunity. Orange
is great for stimulation and motivation; it hones and builds
focused energy. Orange is also great for lucidity and orderliness.
Carnelian, in the family of orange crystals, is the stone to wear
if you are embarking on a new exercise regimen or training for a
sporting event. Any orange stone will help keep the physical and
emotional self in balance. Some parents have reported great
effects after giving a child who was a finicky eater a carnelian to
wear. If you are feeling a bit depressed or missing some of your
general lust for life, wear an orange stone. You will snap out of
it right away!

The saffron orange robes of Buddhist monks reflect divine
life, as do the orange velvet crosses of the Knights of the Holy
Ghost. Roman brides wore vials of orange to indicate the eter-
nalness of their wedding vows.

Yellow

Yellow relates to the solar plexus chakra and to personal power, freedom, control, fire, and the eyes. Emotionally, yellow rules the intellect. For healing, yellow is clarity. If you are in a career that necessitates good communication, place a big chunk of yellow quartz on your bookshelf in your office; this will create a cheerful energy and kindle your desire to be in contact. You should wear citrine, topaz, or yellow zircon to improve your ability to speak clearly and with ease. Or, if you are shy, yellow amber will help you to open up and share. These yellow stones will also make life more enjoyable for they are harbingers of happiness. Yellow is also a color that encourages honesty. Wearing yellow crystals as jewelry during your working day will help you and your coworkers on a daily basis.

Green

Green relates to the heart chakra and to relationships, the heart and lungs, the element of air, the sense of touch, and the will for life. Soulwise, it is the caring nurturer and the healer. In healing, it helps with balance and overall health and well-being. Green stones are among the most loved. It is easy to see why because they offer so much emotional soothing. Emerald and green jade bring security, prosperity, and protection. Other green stones, such as chrysocolla and malachite, calm the mind, and green-flecked bloodstone can serve as a stress buffer.

Alchemists taught that the light of the emerald reveals the most closely guarded of all secrets. In medieval times, physicians wore green cloaks as they worked with herbs to develop cures. It is still the color preferred by pharmacologists. Green is the color associated with the wood element in Chinese astrology. For Muslims, green is the emblem of salvation. In medieval times, painters portrayed Christ's cross in green, as it was the instrument by which the human race was regenerated through his great sacrifice. Green stones have a large role in the Arthurian and Holy Grail legends.

Blue

Blue relates to the throat chakra and to communication, intuition, listening, and the ears. Soulwise, blue is the teacher. For healing, it maintains calm and protects the aura. I have to admit to a preference, above all, for blue stones. We all need to pay attention to such affinities, as they express much about our psyches. Blue is the color of creativity and mind control. To embark on any creative and intellectually demanding project, try wearing a lovely ring or pendant of blue lace agate. If you are feeling like you might be obsessing over something or overly influenced by someone else's thoughts and opinions, try sodalite, one of the stones relegating independence of mind. The beautiful blue sapphire is also great for making personal declarations of independence and for feeling good about yourself while you make them.

To Tibetan Buddhists and to the Egyptians, the color blue has represented transcendent wisdom; it is truth. For Christians, blue and white are the colors of Mary, Our Lady, and of detachment from the material world. In Poland, the houses of brides-to-be are painted blue.

Indigo

Indigo relates to the third eye and to intuition. Emotionally, it corresponds to the urge toward the spiritual. For healing, it opens the third eye and promotes clear-headedness.

Violet

Violet relates to the crown chakra and connection to all else in the universe. Emotionally, it is the deep connection to spirit. For healing, it works on deep tissue and helps rid oneself of deep pain. Gentle purple amethyst is good for issues of sensitivity. Amethyst can help keep energy from draining out of you. Many people drink too much because they are sensitive to environmental noise and are trying to block out some of the overstimulation. Another reason for substance abuse is the longing for an ecstatic spiritual experience. Use amethyst and see if you see a difference in these situations. The purplish agates will also guard the receptive nature and act as ballasts for stability and contentment. Violet is associated with secrecy, the veil behind which transformation takes place.

Brown, Gray, Black, White, Silver, and Gold

These colors are not chakra colors but certainly exist in the world of crystals and stones. Ancient Romans and the Catholic Church regarded brown as the color of humility and poverty—thus the brown robes for monastic orders. Brown is a color representing safety and the home. Brown gems and rocks are great stability stones. Agate, jasper, and petrified wood all act as agents of security.

The ancient Egyptians regarded gray as the color of fertility. The color symbolized resurrection in medieval times, and the artists of that era depicted Jesus at the Last Judgment in robes of gray, the color of grief and mourning. Gray, you may be interested to learn, is the first color the human eye can perceive after birth.

Black relates to issues of protection and strength. If psychic vampires who rob your energy are surrounding you, wear jet or onyx or obsidian. This color also girds your personal energies and gives you more inner authority. In North Africa, black symbolizes the color of the life-giving rich earth and of nourishing rain clouds. Christian and Muslim clergy wear black robes to proclaim their renunciation of all vanity and show their faith. Sufi dervishes see the progress of the inner life as a ladder of color, starting at the lowest rung of white and ascending to the highly evolved black, the color to which all other colors lead.

White represents purity, peace, patience, and protection; silver relates to communication and greater access to the universe; and gold is a direct connection to God and facilitates wealth and ease.

Increasing the Beneficial Powers of Stones

Crystals and gems have specific correspondences with different astrological signs. This part of gem science was developed by the Chaldeans of long ago. The stones will have optimal effect if they are worn according to their correlating astrological sign. For example, Cancers can wear pearls to express and protect their sensitive inner natures. The effect will be even greater when the Sun is in Cancer, and greatest of all when the Moon is in Cancer too. Scorpios will be even more powerful than usual when sporting rubies during their birth month, and so on.

By the same token, gems and crystals vibrate to different numbers. Each letter of the alphabet is associated with a number, as indicated by the following chart:

1	2	3	4	5	6	7	8	9
a	b	c	d	e	f	g	h	i
j	k	l	m	n	o	p	q	r
s	t	u	v	w	x	y	z	

Here is an example of how you can use gemstones and numbers. The name Brenda adds up to the number 26 ($2 + 9 + 5 + 5 + 4 + 1$), which in turn adds up to 8 ($2 + 6$). Thus, Brenda could work with and wear jet, a stone corresponding to the number 8. And if Brenda happens to be a Capricorn—the astrological sign corresponding to jet (see the table on the following page)—the stone's beneficial effects will be even more pronounced.

Number	Stone or Metal	Corresponding Sign(s)
1	Aquamarine	Aries, Gemini, Pisces
	Beryl	Leo
	Copper	Taurus, Sagittarius
	Obsidian	Sagittarius
	Turquoise	Scorpio, Sagittarius, Pisces
2	Garnet	Leo, Virgo, Capricorn, Aquarius
	Sapphire	Virgo, Libra, Sagittarius
	Tourmaline	Libra
3	Amber	Leo, Aquarius
	Amethyst	Virgo, Capricorn, Aquarius, Pisces
	Aventurine	Aries
	Herkimer diamond	Sagittarius
	Lapis lazuli	Sagittarius
	Ruby	Cancer, Leo, Scorpio, Sagittarius
4	Bloodstone	Aries, Libra, Pisces
	Emerald	Aries, Taurus, Gemini
	Moonstone	Cancer, Libra, Scorpio
	Quartz	All
	Sodalite	Sagittarius
	Tiger's-eye	Capricorn
5	Amazonite	Virgo
	Carnelian	Taurus, Cancer, Leo
	Peridot	Leo, Virgo, Scorpio, Sagittarius
6	Apache tear	Aries
	Bloodstone	Aries, Libra, Pisces
	Carnelian	Taurus, Cancer, Leo
	Cat's-eye	Aries, Taurus, Capricorn
	Citrine	Aries, Leo, Libra
	Moldavite	Scorpio
	Onyx	Leo
	Peridot	Leo, Virgo, Scorpio, Sagittarius
7	Agate	Gemini
	Pearl	Gemini, Cancer
	Peridot	Leo, Virgo, Scorpio, Sagittarius
	Rose quartz	Taurus, Libra
8	Chrysolite	Taurus
	Jet	Capricorn
	Opal	Cancer, Libra, Scorpio
9	Hematite	Aries, Aquarius
	Malachite	Scorpio, Capricorn

3

Crystal Lore A–Z

Following is a veritable encyclopedia of crystals and their special qualities. Remember, crystal healing requires conscious awareness on the part of the user. You must be aware of the potential of a given stone and wear it mindfully.

Amethyst—The Rose de France

The Chinese have been wearing amethyst for more than 8,000 years. Tibetans consider this stone to be sacred to Buddha and make prayer beads from it. One lovely legend associated with the purple crystal is from Greece. It is said that Bacchus, the Greek god of wine, had been angered by some mere mortals. Bacchus vowed a violent death—by tiger—to the very next mortal he encountered. As it happened, a pretty girl by the name of Amethyst was on route to worship at the temple of Diana. The goddess Diana protected Amethyst by turning her into a clear crystal quartz so she could not be torn apart by the ravaging tiger. Bacchus regretted his actions and anointed Amethyst with his sacred wine, bringing her back to life. However, he didn't pour enough to cover her entirely, leaving her legs without color. Thus, amethyst is usually uneven in its purple color. Amethyst's anointment with wine relates to this stone's power to help maintain sobriety. The Greek word *amethystos* means "without wine."

Amethyst is a purple quartz found most commonly in Brazil, Canada, and East Africa. The color can range from light violet to deep purple or can be nearly colorless. Amethyst has been prized for jewelry for hundreds of years, and before a huge cache was discovered in South America, it was valued as a precious gemstone. It is now classified as semiprecious.

It is one of the stones most esteemed by healers. The legendary American psychic Edgar Cayce recommended it for control and temperance. Amethyst is believed to aid in the production of hormones and regulate the circulatory, immune, and metabolic systems. Amethyst is treasured for its centering and calming properties and seems to connect directly to the mind, fighting emotional swings and depression. Aquarians and Pisceans can count it as their birthstone, and this might be a very good thing because the Fishes frequently struggle with substance-abuse issues, and amethyst can conquer drinking and other sensory indulgences, such as out-of-control sexuality. Amethyst also helps with mental focus, intuition, meditation, and memory.

In the early Renaissance, amethyst was held to have the power to prevent evil, at least evil thoughts, and to offer protection in time of war. In the Victorian era, a paler amethyst was called Rose de France and was a favorite stone in jewelry. The Victorians sometimes left amethysts out in the sun to fade them. Nowadays, the darker purple stones are considered much more valuable. This lovely purple gem continues to reign as one of the most popular of all stones. Little wonder, since it is such an aid to our physical and emotional health.

Aquamarine—Seawater Stone

A favorite among sailors and mariners, it is said that this stone will keep you safe. Aquamarine is the signifier of the oceanic divinities, sea goddesses, and sirens. The Egyptians loved this gem and gifted it to the dead as part of a treasure hoard that would grant them safety in the next life. They also gifted it to the gods of the netherworld as a guarantee of safe passage. Egyptian high priests wore two aquamarines, or *shoham*, as they called them, on their shoulders engraved with the names of the six tribes of Egypt. This sacred stone was also one of the twelve sanctified gems used in the breastplate of the biblical King Solomon. Today, aquamarine can be a boon to a couple, as it helps maintain a long and happy marriage. And it defends against the devil! The sun is the nemesis of the blue gem because the color of aquamarine fades if overexposed to sunlight.

Beryl—Stone of Power

Medieval historian Arnoldus Saxo said that warriors used beryl to help in battle and also reported that it was good for court cases. Saxo was perhaps a bit hyperbolic in his declaration that the wearer of this stone was made unconquerable and smarter and cured of any laziness! Thomas de Cantimpre's German classic *De Proprietatibus Rerum* spoke about the power of beryl to reawaken the love of married couples. Early crystal balls were frequently made of beryl polished into spheres, rather like J. R. R. Tolkien's palantirs used by wizards. The Druids and Celts used beryl to divine the future, and legend has it that Merlin, King Arthur's magician, carried a beryl ball around with him for exactly that purpose. Beryl still has a well-earned reputation as the stone of power. Beryl is a blue, green, white, red, or yellow prismatic stone, and can be found in India, Brazil, the Czech Republic, Norway, France, Russia, and North America. The aforementioned aquamarine is a beryl, as is the precious emerald. These two members of the beryl family are much better known than beryl itself, but beryl is one of the most important gem minerals. Beryl is colorless in its pure form, which is called goshenite, and gains its lovely colorations through impurities. So, when one is talking about emerald, it is simply green beryl; aquamarine is blue beryl. Pink beryl is morganite, and yellow-green beryl is heliodor. To confuse the issue (or perhaps not), red beryl is referred to as red beryl, and golden beryl is called exactly that.

Beryl has a most unusual and important healing asset—it prevents people from doing the unnecessary. Further, it helps the wearers focus and remove distractions, and therefore is said to help people become calmer and more positive. Beryl also strengthens the liver, kidneys, and intestines, as well as the pulmonary and circulatory systems. It is especially effective for the throat, and pulverized beryl can be mixed into an elixir specifically for this reason. Some crystal healers use beryl along with lapis lazuli as a sedative for nervous conditions. If you get overwhelmed at work or have a huge task ahead of you, efficiency-enhancing beryl will get you through it.

Bloodstone—Martyr's Stone

In medieval times, Christians used bloodstone for sculptured bas-reliefs depicting the martyred saints and Christ's crucifixion—thus the name "martyr's stone." The myth behind bloodstone is that some of Christ's blood dripped down and stained some jasper that lay at the foot of the cross. The great Louvre Museum in Paris holds the seal of Holy Roman Emperor Rudolf II carved into bloodstone. The ancient Egyptians loved bloodstone and gifted it to pharaohs, great warriors, and kings, believing it had the power to calm their tempers and prevent wrath and bloodshed.

An ancient book of Egyptian magic, known as *The Leyden Papyrus*, recorded the high regard for bloodstone: "The world has no greater thing; if any one have this with him he will be given whatever he asks for; it also assuages the wrath of kings and despots, and whatever the wearer says will be believed. Whoever bears this stone, which is a gem, and pronounces the name engraved upon it, will find all doors open while bonds and stone walls will be rent asunder."

Damigeron, a classical historian, wrote that bloodstone could disclose the future through what were called audible oracles and could also change the weather. He further claimed that this favored stone kept the mind sharp and the body healthy and protected the reputation of anyone who wore it.

Calcite—Bone of the Earth

The ancients believed that calcite placed at the base of a pyramid could amplify the structure's power.

Carnelian—Safety Stone

Jafar, the ancient Egyptian religious leader, said, "He who wears carnelian will have whatever he desires." Wearing carnelian dates back to at least biblical times; there are several mentions of soldiers and priests wearing it. Carnelian was a favorite in ancient and medieval times, when people believed that wearing the stone could protect them against injury from falling stones. As the saying goes, "No man who wore a carnelian was ever found in a collapsed house or beneath a fallen wall." Other lore includes the Armenian belief that an elixir of powdered carnelian would lift any cloud and fill the heart with happiness. In olden days, carnelian was credited with being able to defy no less than the devil. So, people wore this lovely red-orange stone to protect themselves from evil, oftentimes repeating this prayer:

In the name of God the Just, the very Just!
I implore you, O God, King of the World,
God of the World, deliver us from the Devil
Who tries to do harm and evil to us
Through bad people and from the evil of the envious.

If you have lost your lust for life and fallen into a pattern of old habits and uncreative day-to-day drudgery, this is the stone for you. Carnelian, also referred to in bygone days as carbuncle, is a type of quartz from the chalcedony gem family. Among the more abundantly available stones, it is found in Peru, Iceland, Romania, Britain, India, Pakistan, and the Czech Republic. Carnelian is a clear stone and is most commonly thought of as red, thus the name, but also comes in orange and occasionally very dark brown. It is found in pebble form and is translucent.

Carnelian has a long history. It is an earth stone and acts as an anchor to the earth. Carnelian is thought to eliminate fear of death and has a grounding and clarifying effect. In olden days, it was used as a sort of backward mirror to recall historical events. It is a lucky stone for people pursuing business ventures and for women hoping to have children. Carnelian is linked with the lower chakras and can heal holes in the etheric body and give support for letting go of anger, old resentments, and emotions that no longer serve a positive purpose. Orange carnelian is especially beloved for its ability to promote energy and vitality, and to warm the emotions.

Part of the tradition surrounding carnelian is that if worn at your throat it helps you overcome timidity and lends the power of great and eloquent speech. Like some other red stones, carnelian also gives you courage. In addition, wearing carnelian can offer you a sense of comfort with your environment and create the proper atmosphere for meditation and total clarity of mind and thought. Carnelian as a pendant or belt gives you control of your thoughts and understanding of others.

Celestite—Angel Stone

Use this stone to get in contact with your guardian angel. The lore about this sky blue stone is that it is a star seed from the Pleiades, which had sent one hundred million geodes to Earth. It is a truth-telling crystal, rendering anyone holding it unable to tell lies.

Angelite is a condensed form of celestite with a highly unusual pattern of striping that looks like angel wings. Both forms of the magical stone will put you in touch with spirits and helpful energies from the angelic realm.

Celestite takes its name from the heavenly blue color for which it is favored, though its range of hues includes shades of white and yellow. Celestite, mined for its salts and the strontium it contains, has another connection to the sky: it is used in fireworks, where it flames a fiery crimson. Celestite is found most abundantly in the Great Lakes Region of North America as well as in Italy, Germany, and Madagascar. It is sometimes mistaken for its look-alike barite, but a flame test will tell the truth. If the flame is a pale green, the mineral is barite, but if it is red, it is most certainly celestite.

Celestite, which resonates with all the chakras, is most powerful. A geode of celestite crystal is believed to be filled with angel energy and brings the highest consciousness. It is a great balancing stone, creating attunement with high intellect and balance with the male and female energies.

Celestite is the stone to keep with you before any speaking engagements or writing that you need to do. It aids the flow of thoughts and words. Most interestingly of all, it is a "listening stone." Hold a piece of celestite and listen carefully to the voice within; the wisdom from this stone will reveal your deepest intuition and lead you to the right action. Meditation is greatly assisted by this crystal, as it is believed to hold the wisdom of the archangels. In meditation, you can ask celestite for knowledge you need, whether it is a memory of a past life, a vision or an out-of-body experience, and it will be made known to you. Celestite is also a dream stone to keep by your bed for insight into the meaning of your night visions.

Chalcedony—Stone of Protection

Chalcedony, made of Earth's ancient living things, has incredible powers of protection. In the eighteenth century, it was used to chase off bogeymen or anything that went bump in the night. Associated with the Holy Grail, chalcedony was a favorite material for chalices and was believed to provide protection even from poison.

Chrysoberyl—Supernatural Seeing Stone

This little-known gem has two siblings, alexandrite and cat's-eye, that have stolen all the attention away from the lovely but less showy green, yellow, and brown transparent type of chrysoberyl. The stone occurs in Canada, Norway, Australia, Ghana, Burma, the Ural Mountains in Russia, and the other gem havens of Sri Lanka and Brazil. It appears in rare instances as a cyclic crystal that looks to be hexagonal but is a triplet of three twins called a trilling.

Chrysoberyl is also called cymophane and occurs in colorations ranging from honey gold to bright green. It usually comes in a domed cabochon shape. If intense light is shone into it, one side will look milky and the other will remain golden; this is known as the milk-and-honey effect. The *eye effect* is the result of infinitesimal needle-like inclusions that refract light, creating a line of light that runs through the center.

Chrysoberyl has been used to manifest destiny and direct fortune for centuries by enhancing visionary powers, and it makes an excellent talisman. It is also prized by healers because it can double the power of other stones and reveal the causes of illness as well as assist with lowering high cholesterol and the hormonal surges of adrenaline. Chrysoberyl is a crystal used for compassion, forgiveness, and emotional release and has been called the stone of new beginnings. This is one of the few crystals that can enable one to see both sides of an issue and get over blocks and stubbornness. If you are harboring a grudge against a coworker or loved one, chrysoberyl will cut right through the old anger and help you to move on.

Chrysocolla—Heart Chakra Crystal

A green or blue opaque stone, chrysocolla is almost never heard of outside of gem circles. Many people think it is a symbol of Earth due to its blue-and-green planetlike patterning. It is a stone with a gentle energy, unlike many other stones that have intense energy, such as some quartzes, lapis, malachite, and obsidian. It occurs in The Democratic Republic of Congo, Russia, North America, and Chile.

Tranquil chrysocolla is a heart stone that affects the heart chakra, enabling the gentle release of emotions, guilt, and fear. It is a truth stone. It can ease the pain and discomfort of arthritis and other bone or skeletal issues. Ulcers, stomach pain, and intestinal problems are greatly alleviated with this healer.

The stone is associated with Gaia—our Earth Mother—and also Kwan Yin, the benevolent bringer of compassion. Chrysocolla evokes the qualities of these goddesses: nurturing, forgiveness, and tolerance. It is viewed as a lunar stone, perfect for new-moon meditations and meditations on global issues such as the environment and world peace. By holding this placid stone in your hand, you can help send healing energy out to the planet at large.

Egyptians favored chrysocolla as an amulet for protection. This earthy stone can give confidence to the shy and empower them to speak the truth. Thus, chrysocolla would make a wonderful accessory to wear as a choker or near the throat when giving any kind of public speech. This beautifully oceanic rock can also give the wearer a better ability for listening, an all-important component to communication. It amplifies sensitivity to aid in understanding what is spoken as well as unspoken. This generous crystal was traditionally used by musicians for its ability to ease expression and give greater beauty to the singing voice.

Chrysocolla also increases the capacity for love, one of the sweetest and most beneficial qualities any stone can offer. But my favorite feature of chrysocolla is that it tells you when to be silent and when to speak.

Chrysoprase—Love of Truth

Emanuel Swedenborg, a seventeenth-century Swedish theologian, scientist, philosopher, and metaphysician, credited this apple-green chalcedony with giving people a love of the truth. Other lore regarding chrysoprase is that the stone offers a most rare capability to give a man condemned to be hanged a sure escape from his executioner. All he has to do, supposedly, is place this crystal in his mouth.

Emeralds—Popular Protectors

"Almost every high-quality emerald was smuggled at some point in its history," according to *National Geographic*.

Emeralds are believed to have come to Earth from the planet Venus. This precious stone is one of the only ones that retains its value, according to gemologists and jewelers, even if it is deeply flawed. Emeralds have a richly varied mythology attached to their glowing green history. For thousands of years, Hindu physicians in India regarded this stone as a benefit to many stomach-related illnesses—it was an appetite stimulant, a curative for dysentery, a laxative, and a treatment for too much stomach-irritating bile. In India of old, they also believed emeralds could drive away demons or rid a body of ill spirits.

Another ancient belief is that emeralds portend events from the future, rather like scrying, or see things in a mirror or the glassy surface of the gem. Emeralds were thought to be foes to any and all sorcerers, a belief stemming from a legend that emeralds vanquished all wizardry in their wake. The ancients loved emeralds and connected them with the eyes. Theophrastus, a student of Plato's, taught that emeralds protected the eyesight. He was taken so seriously that engravers kept emeralds on their tables to look at to refresh their eyes.

Egyptians valued emeralds almost beyond any other stone and claimed their goddess Isis wore a great emerald. Anyone who looked upon Isis's green jewel was assured of a safe trip to the underworld, the land of the dead. Egypt was the main source for emeralds until the sixteenth century. The Cleopatra mines, south of Cairo, were the mother lode, and emerald traders from as far away as India sought the stones, obtained at great human cost under wretched conditions of extreme heat and dangerous underground shafts. Let's hope that the common belief that these stones also protected people from poison and venomous serpents was true. Emeralds were anathemas to snakes, which would supposedly be struck blind by merely looking upon the stones.

In ancient Rome, emeralds were quite sought after by the wealthy class. Nero watched the games in the Coliseum through a set of priceless spectacles made from emeralds. In the 1500s, with the capture of South America by Pizarro and Cortez, the Spanish made emeralds more available to the Europeans, who had an insatiable appetite for jewels and gold. The discovery in 1558 of the Muzo mine in Colombia uncovered emeralds of incredible beauty and size, prompting the Spanish conquistadors to take over the mine and declare the natives slaves. Perhaps part of Montezuma's revenge involved the seizure of the emerald mines. Emeralds were a popular cure for dysentery in the sixteenth century when worn touching the torso or held in the mouth. As with all very valuable stones, the people who actually mine them have no access to them unless they are smuggled out of the mines. According to a recent article in *National Geographic*, however, this is done more frequently than one might think, especially with larger stones.

Fluorite—Stone of Revelation

Fluorite comes in every color of the rainbow and features a bonus—its fluorescent quality produces a special, rather eerie glow under ultraviolet light. Pure fluorite (with its chemical makeup of fluorine and calcium) is colorless. Colored fluorite—in oceanic green, dark purple, buttery yellow, pale amethyst, or bright blue—results from traces of other elements.

Fluorite is dualistic in its opacity—it can be crystal-clear or translucent. Fluorite is rather like glass except that it's brittle and soft, which keeps it out of the running as a precious gemstone, even though it is just as beautiful to look at and polishes to a brilliant, glossy surface. The yielding surface scratches easily, making it an unfortunate choice for a ring. Fluorite is best worn as an earring, close to the brain and neck and spine, where it offers enormous assistance and healing. Even as a pin or pendant, it must be handled very gingerly to avoid damage or scratches to the surface.

Fluorite is commonly found in China, Peru, Norway, Australia, Britain, and several areas of North America. The state of Illinois has massive fluorite deposits, which formed around 150 million years ago from the fluorinated (by Mother Nature herself) water that was heated and rose to a high level during the Jurassic period, flowing all around limestone deposits from the earlier Mississippian period of 330 million years ago. This fluorine-rich brine hit the calcium-laden limestone, and the conditions were perfect for the crystallization of fluorite. Think about that for a moment. The crystal you hold in your hand may well have formed 100 million years ago. What vast energy must be contained inside!

A Rainbow of Uses for Fluorite

Violet- or amethyst-colored fluorite is especially good for the bones, including bone marrow. It jogs the third eye and, best of all, imparts good old common sense! Green fluorite is favored for its ability to ground and center excessive physical and mental energy. Clear fluorite awakens the crown chakra and lets go of anything holding back spiritual development. Blue fluorite facilitates mental clarity, orderly thought, and the ability to be a master communicator. Yellow fluorite kindles the synapses and awakens memory. It will also make you smarter and boost your creativity a great deal.

Any fluorite reduces electromagnetic pollutants and cleanses the aura. Get a big chunk of fluorite at your favorite metaphysical five-and-dime and put it right beside your computer to decrease stress. Those long hours of staring at the screen will cease to sap your energy. Look at your fluorite at least once an hour to reduce eye and brain strain, too!

Garnet—Noah's Lantern

Garnets are conductors of past-life memories and are memory sharpeners in the here and now. They offer the welcome advantage of increasing patience. Garnets also promote compassion and awareness of the world and the self. They help a person let go of negative beliefs, especially self-loathing.

Garnets have much lore around them. The ancients believed them to have protective powers that prevented travelers from accidents and mishaps and also kept away nightmares and bad dreams. It is said that the fiery glow of a garnet kept Noah and his ark afloat. A popular biblical gem, garnet was one of the stones used by King Solomon in his breastplate. In Asia, garnets were used as bullets, most notably in the rebellion in India in 1892.

Garnet's name comes from the Greek word for pomegranate, and the gem is associated with a Greek myth surrounding this fruit. Persephone, the daughter of Zeus and Demeter, tasted three seeds from the pomegranate, dooming herself to spend half of the year in the underworld, married to Hades, god of the underworld.

Hawk's-Eye—Seer's Stone

Hawk's-eye is an abundance stone. It can look very much like its namesake, the eye of the powerful bird. This underknown crystal is a darker version of tiger's-eye. It occurs in South Africa, North America, India, and Australia and is banded like its brother stone. Hawk's-eye has strong earth energy. It has the rare ability to calm and energize at the same time. While tiger's-eye is about taking in the long view, hawk's-eye is about taking the aerial vantage point, a detached viewpoint.

Hawk's-eye has a blue-green glint, while tiger's-eye is yellow gold. Both offer flashes of insight from different perspectives. In many cultures, hawks are the messengers of the gods. In the same way, you can hold this stone to your third eye or in the palm of your hand and ask for deep wisdom. Wait and listen, and the answer will come to you. I love this stone because it attracts not only wealth and material objects but also people who are good for you and bring advantageous connections. Hawk's-eye is your solace when you are in real trouble and can't see your way out. In healing it is used to strengthen the circulatory system, legs, bowels, and eyes. Photographers, scientists, airline pilots, and anyone whose vision is essential to their success would do well to wear hawk's-eye at work.

Herkimer—Diamond Dreams

First off, this is not a diamond. It is clear quartz first discovered in Herkimer, New York. It was exclusively mined there until recently, when it was uncovered in Oaxaca, Mexico. The reason it is nicknamed diamond is because of its brilliance, sparkle, and diamond shape. It also has a lovely rainbowlike effect at its center—optimism at its very core.

This crystal releases energy blockage and is helpful to the chakras. Herkimer diamond is a stone of attunement. It is most effective if placed upon a chakra area in need of therapy. For example, if you are having difficulty speaking about something that troubles you, place a Herkimer diamond on your throat. If you are brokenhearted, place it on the heart chakra. Some crystal healers believe the greatest power of the Herkimer is the prevention of illness.

This stone has a nearly unmatched ability to bring tremendously meaningful, prophetic, and illuminative dreams. This crystal greatly boosts the intuition and even engenders ease in past-life recollection.

If you place a Herkimer diamond beneath your pillow, you will have incredibly vivid dreams, which you should keep track of in a dream journal and discuss in your dream work. If the power of these dreams is overwhelming, you can make it more manageable by placing an amethyst beside the Herkimer diamond, which will moderate the intensity of the dreams.

Herkimer diamonds are power stones, bringing great vitality and exuberance into your life. They can redirect stress away from you with their absorbing abilities. Placing these stones in your bedroom will cause stress to melt away and help you relax and feel safe.

Lastly, if you live anywhere near a nuclear facility of any kind, whether it is a power station or medical hospital that performs radiation, this stone will absorb the radiation and help protect you and your loved ones. Herkimer diamonds retain the memory imprint of what they have born witness to in their environment and reflect back to us a gentle understanding of what they have seen. I have a Herkimer diamond pendant that evokes many compliments. I was attracted to it at the International New Age Trade Show in Denver a few years ago and couldn't stop thinking about it. Later, when I was diagnosed with breast cancer, to the amazement of my friends and family, I didn't need radiation or chemotherapy, and I think I know why!

Iron Pyrite—The Shaman's Mirror

Iron pyrite, otherwise known as Fool's Gold, was supreme in early Mexico, where it was polished into mirrors for shamanic scrying, a method of looking into the future and the past. These people also carved sacred symbols into these vessels of inter-dimensional viewing.

Jade—Concentrated Essence of Love

Jade has been called the concentrated essence of love. The word jade comes from the Spanish word *piedra de hijada*, translating to "stone of the flank," a name prompted by the Indian use of jade as a cure for kidney disease. Jade also served as an aid to ancient midwives and birth mothers, and on the opposite end of the spectrum of life, the Egyptians, Chinese, and Mayans placed a small piece of jade into the mouths of the dead.

In 1595, the erudite world-exploring nobleman Sir Walter Raleigh wrote this about jade: "These Amazones have likewise great stores of these plates of gold, which they recover by exchange, chiefly for a kind of greene stone, which the Spaniards call Piedras Hijada, and we use for spleene stones and for the disease of the stone we also esteem them. Of these I saw divers in Guiana, and commonly every King or Casique had one, which theire wife for the most part weare, and they esteeme them as great jewels."

Jasper—Building Block of Heaven

According to the Bible, the top of the holy walls of New Jerusalem, or heaven, contain 4,780 bricks encrusted with 1,327 hand-cut, polished red jasper stones. Jasper is mentioned throughout the Bible, particularly as a protective stone in the breastplates of the priests of Aaron. Evidently, the ancients considered it to be an extremely powerful stone. Even God is referred to metaphorically as a red jasper stone in Revelations (4:3), which states, "And He who sat there was like a jasper and a sardius stone in appearance; and there was a rainbow around the throne, in appearance like an emerald."

The ancients also favored jasper for curing snakebites, repelling evil spirits, and bringing rain. "Lithica," a fourth-century epic poem, praises this stone: "The gods propitious hearken to his prayers, who'ever the polished glass-green Jasper wears: His parsed glebe they'll saturate with rain, and send for shower to soak the thirsty plain."

The Bible mentions jasper quite often; the great city of heaven is reputed to have jasper walls.

This opaque kind of chalcedony is a common stone here on Earth. In fact, it is found on every continent. It occurs in shades of brown, yellow, blue, green, and red, as well as combinations of these colors, often displayed in exquisite striations. Jasper has been ground up into powder and added to healing elixirs for thousands of years. The stone offers encouraging effects, but they tend to happen gradually over a long period of time. Patience is required. Jasper is an energy crystal and also a stone of sensuality, engendering immense ardor.

Brown jasper can connect you to the earth and also to past lives, helping with regressional memories and uncovering patterns that have clung on from incarnation to incarnation. If you are interested in exploring previous incarnations, wear brown jasper rings or bracelets on your left arm and pay attention to your dreams, you may be surprised at what will be revealed!

Yellow jasper is the spirit stone, an aid during any spiritual work. It is also a great stone to take on a trip, a traveler's support. Yellow jasper offers vigor and touches upon the endocrine system. Wear a yellow jasper ring on your right hand on your next trip and you will enjoy lively dreams.

Blue jasper impacts the sacral and heart chakras and makes travel in the astral plane possible. This is a powerfully mystical crystal. Blue jasper can put you into the spirit realm yet keep you anchored to the earthly plane. It is perfect for any soul work. If you want to embark on a new spiritual practice or even deepen your meditation, this gem will set you on the proper path.

Green jasper is great for the skin and for the mind; if you are thinking too much about any one thing, green jasper will dispel the obsession. Women value this shade because it prevents bloating. For clear skin and an even clearer mind, wear green jasper!

Red jasper can bring emotions that lie beneath the surface to the forefront for healing. This stone is connected strongly to the root chakra, the source of sexual energy and kundalini. If you would like to explore the sacred sexual practice of tantra, both partners could wear red jasper, the stone of passion. Red jasper can be a tool for rebirth and also for finding justice.

Jasper is a nurturing stone and can create a sense of wholeness through chakra alignment. Now that I think about it, I need to place jasper on my desk, as it is a great organizational crystal and would help see all my various projects through to completion. This is a stone that balances the male and female energies. Jasper will ground you, and the lovely spectrum of shades can help you care for yourself, body and soul.

lapis lazuli—Babylonian Blue

Ancient Babylonians and their south-of-the-Mediterranean neighbors, the Egyptians, could not get enough of this bright blue jewel. The Egyptians named it chesbet and usually included it on their list of VIP items to be paid to nations under the dominion of the great kingdom of the Nile. The Babylonians, who piled lapis lazuli high in their tributes to Egypt, had access to a plenitude of this stone because they were the earliest people to mine it—back in 4000 B.C.!

Lapis lazuli was so holy to the Egyptians that the high priest himself wore a pendant of the blue stone in the shape of their goddess of truth, Mat. The Egyptians seemingly wished to swim in seas of lapis, as they used it daily—as adornment, for funeral masks and tools, and as an ingredient in their art. Lapis has the unusual ability to hold its pigment even when it is ground up, helpful to artists and Egyptians like Cleopatra who used it as eyeshadow.

Magnetite—Herculean Stone

The ancients were fascinated with magnetite and its mysterious workings. The great Pliny wrote that the first instance of the discovery of magnetite, commonly known as lodestone, happened when a Cretan shepherd was walking on Mount Ida with his flock and the nails of his shoes clung to a rock in the field. The shepherd's name was Magnes. Pliny also recorded the tale of Ptolemy, who wished to make an iron statue of a woman for a temple dedicated to his wife and his sister. The trick was that he wanted to use the new art of magnetism to suspend the statue in air without any visible means of support! Unfortunately for us, Ptolemy and his architect, the Alexandrian Dinocrates, died before its completion. Otherwise, there might have been an eighth wonder of the world.

Lodestone, the polarized version of magnetite, was held to be a protection against spells and other magical mischief. The ancients also believed that a small piece of lodestone beneath the pillow would ensure virtue. Alexander the Great gave his soldiers lodestone to defend against unseen evil spirits.

Malachite—Stone of Juno

This striped green stone belonged to the Greek goddess Venus. The Greeks believed it had magical powers when set in copper jewelry. The Romans switched things around a bit and turned malachite over to Juno, cutting it into triangular shapes to indicate her sacred peacock symbol. My favorite bit of malachite lore is that drinking from a goblet cut from this stone supposedly gave the imbiber an understanding of the language of animals!

Moonstone—Prophecy and Passion

In olden times, it was believed that wearing a moonstone during the waning moon would offer prophetic abilities. For thousands of years, the people of India have believed that moonstone was holy. They would only display the stone on a cloth of yellow, the most spiritual color in their culture. The Indians also believed moonstone was very potent in the bedroom and not only aroused enormous passion but also gave lovers the ability to read their future together. The only problem was that they had to hold the moonstone in their mouths during the full moon to enjoy these magical properties.

Opal—Cupid's Stone

In the classical era, people believed that opals were pieces of rainbows that had fallen to the ground. They also dubbed this exquisite iridescent gem Cupid's stone because they felt it looked like the love god's skin. The Arabs believed opals fell from heaven in bright flashes of lightning, thus gaining their amazing fire and color play. The Romans saw opals as symbols of purity and optimism. They believed this stone could protect people from diseases. The Roman name for opal is beautiful and evocative—*cupid paederos*, meaning "a child as beautiful as love."

Saint Albert the Great was one of the most learned men of the thirteenth century, a student of the natural sciences as well as theology, literature, and languages. He fancied mineralogy and waxed on about the opal: "The porphanus is a stone which is in the crown of the Roman Emperor, and none like it has ever been seen; for this very reason it is called porphanus. It is of a subtle vinous tinge, and its hue is as though pure white snow flashed and sparkled with the color of bright, ruddy wine and was overcome by this radiance. It is a translucent stone, and there is a tradition that, formerly, it shone in the nighttime, but now, in our age, it does not sparkle in the dark, it is said to guard the regal honor."

Opals had many superstitions attached to them. There was the belief that an opal wrapped in a bay-laurel leaf could cure any eye disease and combat weak hearts and infection. In the Middle Ages, opal was called *ophthalmios*, or "eye stone." The great Scandinavian epic the E*dda* contained verses about a stone forged by the smithy of the gods to form the eyes of children, doubtless a reference to opal. In olden days, it was thought that an opal would change color according to the mood and health of the owner, going dull and colorless when the owner died. Blond women favored opals because they believed they could keep their hair light in color. I trust they were not using black or dark blue opals!

It was even believed that an opal could render the wearer invisible, making this the patron stone of thieves. Black opal has always had top ranking among opals, being the most rare and dramatic. One legend told that if a love relationship were con-summated with one party wearing a black opal, the gem would soak up the passion and store it in its glow.

Pearls—Tears of the Gods

Pearls have a romantic past. The Chinese regarded them as the physical manifestation of the souls of oysters. One of the pret-tier names given to the pearl was *margarithe*, meaning "child of light." The Arabs called them tears of the gods and said they were formed when raindrops fell into oyster shells. In India, pearls were the perfect wedding gift, promising devotion and fertility. A Hindu wedding ritual involved the piercing of the perfect pearl, a virginity ceremony.

One less-than-successful cure for the plague was this ancient recipe: six grains of powdered pearl in water mixed with ash-tree sap. One remedy for excessive bleeding was a glass of water with one part burned pearl powder. Snuffing the same was a treatment for headaches. Pearl oil was used for nervous conditions, and pearl poultice was even used for leprosy! Other less glamorous uses for pearl potions were treatments for hemorrhoids and poisoning. An elixir made with one-half of a pearl grain was supposed to cure impotence and be an overall aphrodisiac. In bygone days, people were so fond of grinding up pearls that they even used them in toothpaste.

Peridot—Pele's Teardrop

Peridot is one of the most misunderstood gems on the planet. It is really a combination of two other stones, fayalite and forsterite, with a bit of iron, a dash of nickel, and a pinch of chromium. The world's oldest source of the green charmer was the mist-shrouded desert island of Zeberget, also called Saint John's Island, off Egypt's coast. Unfortunately for the peridot miners, this island was a haven for venomous snakes! The pharaohs so treasured their peridot that any uninvited visitors to the island were put to death. It is believed that Cleopatra, queen of the Nile, adorned herself with high-quality peridot instead of emeralds. Nowadays, the only residents of Zeberget are a few turtles and some seabirds.

Now that the mines on Zeberget are no more, most peridot is mined by Native Americans in Arizona and in the exotic locales of Myanmar, Sri Lanka, and the Kashmir Himalayas. Peridot has also been found in some meteorites. In the 1920s, a farmer in Kansas awoke one morning to find lumps of peridot-studded meteorite in his fields. Maybe you really have to follow the peridot road to get to Oz!

Peridot was one of the twelve stones believed to have the power to create miracles for the rituals of these priests and to help protect them in battle. It's possible that the stones from the breastplate of Solomon and his high priest, Aaron, came from this odd little island. And Solomon drank *soma* (an intoxicating plant juice) from cups carved from peridot, thus gaining his wealth of wisdom.

The Romans called peridot the evening emerald. The stone, brought back as booty by the Knights Templars and Crusaders, was used to adorn cathedrals in medieval times. On the Shrine of the Three Magi in Germany's Cologne Cathedral, there is a huge 200-carat peridot.

The powers of peridot are believed to be twice as strong if it is set in gold. Peridot was thought to have the power to drive away evil, and if you are so lucky as to have a goblet carved out of peridot, any medicine you might drink out of it will have magical healing powers. In Hawaii, the lore of this gem is that the goddess Pele cried tears that turned into peridot.

Ruby—Mother of the Earth's Blood

In the tenth century, Chinese gem carvers engraved depictions of dragons and snakes on the surfaces of rubies to gain money and power. Rubies were also used by the Chinese to pay homage to Buddha. In India, worshipers gave rubies as an offering to their god Krishna.

In his famed *Lapidary*, Philippe de Valois lavished praise on the royally red rock, writing that "the books tell us the beautiful clear and fine ruby is the lord of stones; it is the gem of gems and surpasses all other precious stones in virtue." Sir John Mandeville similarly evoked his opinion that ownership of a ruby would accord safety from all peril and wonderful relations with friends and neighbors. He further recommended that rubies be worn on the left side of the body.

In Myanmar, ruby was viewed as a stone of invincibility, and soldiers had a radical approach to harnessing its protective power—before marching into battle, they would embed the gem in their skin! They believed the color "ripened" inside the earth. Prehistoric peoples believed that rubies were crystallized drops of the mother of the earth's blood.

Sapphire—Eye of Horus

The ancient Persians believed that Earth rested on a giant sapphire and the blue sky was a reflection of its color. The Greeks identified white sapphire with the god Apollo. They deemed this stone very important indeed: the oracles at Delphi used it to make their prophecies. The Egyptians designated sapphire as the eye of Horus. Star sapphire is especially prized, as the lines crossing the blue of the stone were believed to represent faith, hope, and charity.

Sapphire has been used as an eye cure for millennia. Medieval scientist Sir Albert the Great recorded incidents in which he had seen sapphire used with success in healing, stating that is was necessary for the stone to be dipped in cold water prior to surgery, and afterward as well. A contemporary of Albert the Great by the name of von Helmont advocated using sapphire as a remedy for plague boils by rubbing the gem on the afflicted spots. He did offer the disclaimer that the condition could not be too advanced and explained the science behind his cure with the early theory of magnetism, in which a force in the sapphire pulled "the pestilential virulence and contagious poison from the infected part."

Magicians and seers love this stone because it adds to their sensitivities and enables them to augur better. Historically, sapphire was regarded as a gem of nobility, and any regal personage wearing this gem would be protected from harm, particularly from the threat of poison. Another legend, though perhaps not very credible, is that Moses wrote the Ten Commandments on tablets of sapphire, but it is more likely that they would have been carved into the soft and more readily available lapis lazuli. Even with God on his side, one wonders where would Moses have gotten sapphires of such massive size and flatness! Sapphire remained popular with the religious; one notable instance was when the twelfth-century bishop of Rennes commended this gem as an ecclesiastical ring due to its connection with the heavens above. The holy- and legal-minded also favored this stone, as it was believed to help counteract deception. Once, sapphires were believed to have gender. Dark sapphires were "male," and light stones were "female."

Star Sapphire—Giver of Great Luck

Sir Richard Burton always carried a star sapphire with him as his talisman while he traveled through Asia and the Middle East. According to Burton, the stone brought him excellent horses and ensured that he received attention right when he needed it. It does seem to have worked, as he is still receiving accolades and consideration long after his passing. A generous soul, he would show his star sapphire to the friendly folk who had helped him, since this gem is a giver of great luck.

Topaz—Saint Hildegard's Cure

Sailors once used this golden gem to shed light on the water during moonless nights. Topaz was also used as an aphrodisiac and to prevent the excesses of love, functions that certainly don't seem to go together. Ground into a dust and mixed with rose water, topaz was used to treat excessive bleeding. Similarly, powdered topaz mixed with wine was a treatment for insanity once upon a time. The ancients used topaz to guard against magicians by setting it in a gold bracelet and wearing it on the left arm. Saint Hildegard of Bingen, who suggested topaz was an aid to poor vision, placed the stone in wine for three straight days and then gently rubbed it on the eye. The wine could then be drunk—after removing the stone, of course. Hers is one of the first written records of a gem elixir. Medieval physicians also used topaz to treat the plague and its accompanying sores, and several miracles were attributed to a particular stone that had been in the possession of Pope Clement VI and Pope Gregory II.

Turquoise—Turkish Stone

One pretty legend relating to turquoise is that rainbows touching the earth generate it. Turquoise seems to have always had a mythic link to horses, beginning with the medieval belief that anyone wearing this stone would be protected from falling off the animal. Sir John Mandeville's *Lapidaire* further claimed that this blue-green stone prevented horses from the harm of drinking cold water when they were sweating and hot. Turkish equestrians went so far as to attach this crystal to the bridles of their horses as a talisman for the animals.

An unusual story about turquoise comes from the court of Emperor Rudolph II, whose physician was given a specimen that had faded completely. The doctor's father had given it to him with these words of wisdom, "Son, as the virtues of the turquoise are said to exist only when the stone has been given, I will try its efficacy by bestowing it upon thee." The young man set it in a ring and in one month's time, the splendid color was completely restored.

Zircon—Legacy of Hyacinth

Blue zircon is a thread of the fabric of Greek mythology. In the tale of the Greek youth Hyacinth, a blue hyacinth flower grew in the place where he died. In a less charming but equally fascinating fable, zircon was used for exorcism. The methodology was simple—a cross was cut into a loaf of freshly baked wheat bread. Then, a zircon was used to trace along the cross shape before the bread was eaten to drive away the evil spirits.

About the Authors

Sibyl Ferguson was a psychic and clairvoyant schoolteacher who died ca.1982. Her published works include *Crystal Ball* and many introductions to the works of Gerald Massey.

Witch Bree is a medievalist, a poet, and a scholar of all things metaphysical, from herbalism to tarot to gemology. A practicing Wiccan and astrologer, she is a member of the Women's Spirituality Forum, founded by Z Budapest. The author of the Witch's Brew book series, Bree leads workshops in northern California.

To Our Readers

Weiser Books, an imprint of Red Wheel/Weiser, publishes books across the entire spectrum of occult and esoteric subjects. Our mission is to publish quality books that will make a difference in people's lives without advocating any one particular path or field of study. We value the integrity, originality, and depth of knowledge of our authors.

Our readers are our most important resource, and we appreciate your input, suggestions, and ideas about what you would like to see published. Please feel free to contact us, to request our latest book catalog, or to be added to our mailing list.

Red Wheel/Weiser, LLC
P.O. Box 612
York Beach, ME 03910-0612
www.redwheelweiser.com